Low-Code Development with Appsmith

Building Internal Tools and Business Applications

Rahul Sharma
Rajat Arora

Apress®

Low-Code Development with Appsmith: Building Internal Tools and Business Applications

Rahul Sharma
Delhi, Delhi, India

Rajat Arora
Delhi, India

ISBN-13 (pbk): 978-1-4842-9812-1
https://doi.org/10.1007/978-1-4842-9813-8

ISBN-13 (electronic): 978-1-4842-9813-8

Managing Director, Apress Media LLC: Welmoed Spahr
Acquisitions Editor: Divya Modi
Development Editor: James Markham
Copy Editor: April Rondeau

Cover designed by eStudioCalamar

Cover image by Pixabay (www.pixabay.com)

Distributed to the book trade worldwide by Apress Media, LLC, 1 New York Plaza, New York, NY 10004, U.S.A. Phone 1-800-SPRINGER, fax (201) 348-4505, email orders-ny@springer-sbm.com, or visit www.springeronline.com. Apress Media, LLC is a California LLC and the sole member (owner) is Springer Science + Business Media Finance Inc (SSBM Finance Inc). SSBM Finance Inc is a **Delaware** corporation.

For information on translations, please e-mail booktranslations@springernature.com; for reprint, paperback, or audio rights, please e-mail bookpermissions@springernature.com.

Apress titles may be purchased in bulk for academic, corporate, or promotional use. eBook versions and licenses are also available for most titles. For more information, reference our Print and eBook Bulk Sales web page at http://www.apress.com/bulk-sales.

Any source code or other supplementary material referenced by the author in this book is available to readers on GitHub (https://github.com/Apress). For more detailed information, please visit https://www.apress.com/gp/services/source-code.

Paper in this product is recyclable

Table of Contents

About the Authors

Rahul Sharma is an architect with 18 years of experience developing Java/J2EE and Python applications. He has worked in a variety of organizations ranging from enterprises to startups. He has experience with various architectures, including monolith, distributed, big data, and streaming.

Rajat Arora is a hands-on programmer with over ten years of experience building software in the fintech domain. He has worked with both monolith and microservices-based architectures using .NET and Java technology stacks. He is currently working as an engineering manager.

About the Technical Reviewer

Arun Verma has been working in the IT industry for more than a decade. He is currently working as a lead engineer and has experience in creating and executing innovative software solutions. He is passionate about utilizing serverless and microservices-based architecture to enhance business productivity and end-to-end project management, from concept through to development and delivery.

Acknowledgments

I am deeply grateful to the many individuals who made this book possible. Each and every one of them played an important role in its success. I want to express my sincere appreciation to Divya Modi for entrusting us with this wonderful opportunity. Her belief in our project provided the foundation for its eventual success.

I also extend my thanks to Shonmirin P. A. for her unwavering dedication and editorial expertise. Her guidance and support were essential in bringing this project to fruition. I am equally grateful to Arun Verma and Mark Powers for their insightful feedback, which helped us refine our ideas and effectively convey our message.

Rajat Arora, my co-author, also deserves special recognition for his vast knowledge and expertise. Our collaborative brainstorming sessions were instrumental in shaping the final product and conveying a clear and concise message.

I would also like to express my gratitude to my loving family—my supportive parents; my wife, Swati; and my children, Rudra and Pranshi— whose unwavering encouragement and patience were essential sources of strength and inspiration throughout this project.

Lastly, I would like to thank my friends, whose insights and knowledge were invaluable in shaping my understanding of the subject matter. Our discussions and debates served as an important benchmark and helped ensure the accuracy and relevance of our ideas.

Introduction

In today's digital landscape, adopting low-code development platforms has become crucial for businesses of all sizes. This approach offers a host of advantages, such as speed, ease of use, and visual interfaces, all while reducing expenses and increasing flexibility. According to a report by Forrester, low-code development can accelerate software development up to ten times faster than the traditional methods. By adopting this approach, businesses can reap a plethora of benefits, including the ability for individuals to create new innovations and facilitate better collaboration across teams. In essence, low-code development platforms offer a practical solution for organizations looking to stay ahead of the curve in this fast-paced digital era.

Appsmith is one such low-code platform that has seen widespread popularity in recent years. It is an open-source platform with a strong community and numerous integrations, offering a variety of tools for delivering business solutions quickly. This book serves as an introduction to Appsmith, and will explain its usefulness and explore its features to establish a foundation for development. Readers will gain hands-on skills for handling errors, debugging, and troubleshooting with Appsmith. Additionally, they will learn efficient monitoring and authentication methods for deploying production-ready systems. Through examples, realistic scenarios, and explanations of necessary tools, this book will help readers gain practical skills for building successful low-code apps.

This book is tailored to business analysts and citizen developers with a technical background who aspire to start developing apps with Appsmith. It will also be helpful for experienced developers seeking to learn a new tool or platform, as well as anyone interested in designing technical solutions with minimal programming. Basic knowledge of object-oriented programming and JavaScript is assumed.

CHAPTER 1

Introduction to Appsmith

Software development without coding has been the principal of various application development paradigms. There have been several attempts to build commercially variable solutions, like computer-aided software design (CASE) tools, rapid application development (RAD), fourth-generation programming languages (4GL), etc. All of these solutions were aimed at solving the issue of organizational productivity. Several organizations adopted these tools to build products quickly and with adequate quality.

All the approaches just mentioned have struggled to deliver on their promises. These tools were expensive, to begin with. Moreover, the applications were complex to develop and challenging to maintain in the long run. Organizations were also required to train and retrain employees to use the tool effectively. The tools were also limited in their capabilities and often failed to perform as predicted. These challenges led to the tools' having very little commercial impact.

Over the last decade, businesses have been going through digital transformations. Moreover, the Covid-19 pandemic has accelerated the need for these transformations. The shortage of skilled developers and the unsatisfactory quality of software development has formed a chasm between software demand and supply chain. This gap has forced companies to reorganize their value chains or even to change their

© Rahul Sharma and Rajat Arora 2023
R. Sharma and R. Arora, *Low-Code Development with Appsmith*,
https://doi.org/10.1007/978-1-4842-9813-8_1

business models, which in turn requires them to rebuild their processes and products in software. Therefore, tools and methods to increase the efficiency of implementing business software are needed like never before.

Low-code Movement

Global market research company Forrester coined the term "low-code development platform (LCDP)" in their 2014 market trend report. As per the original report, LCDP is a software development environment that enables users to develop applications through graphical user interfaces (GUIs) instead of writing code in a traditional programming language. The platform also provides capabilities, maybe GUIs, across the entire software development life cycle (SDLC) spectrum. These capabilities result in faster go-to-market products and reduced overall cost of maintenance.

Similar to its predecessors, like CASE and RAD tools, low-code platforms are built on the concepts of abstractions where the user can directly express business processes and requirements without getting mired in coding details. While originally intended for applications involving databases, business processes, content management systems, and web interfaces, LCDPs have matured enough to develop almost all applications except for embedded or high-performance applications, such as games or scientific computing. LCDP is now used to create applications with the prominent characteristics discussed in the following sections.

Ease of Use

Almost all LCDPs are GUI-based platforms with what-you-see-is-what-you-get (WYSIWYG) editors. The editor offers several functions, such as drag-and-drop facilities, pre-built templates, data capabilities like bar charts and filters, decision engines for building logic, and form builders for data capture. Domain-specific LCDPs offer domain modeling capabilities that can be used to generate and maintain their respective use cases.

LCDPs often have some aspects of workflow management. Generic LCDPs provide limited capabilities for such purposes. However, LCDPs of the workflow management domain focus on the visual design of workflows with additional support for workflow execution and third-party connections.

All these features are targeted to simplify the complexity of building software. In turn, they also empower a non-programmer to generate applications for business needs. To succeed at this goal, the platform must provide representations that its users can follow intuitively without investing in massive training.

Speed of Delivery

Production rollout can pose several challenges. Applications must be validated against specifications and deployed on infrastructure with the required governance. Bypassing these rules can be a severe risk for an organization's information technology (IT) setup. Thus, most LCDPs provide runtime environments that package the application in a specified format. The low-code runtime allows for immediate testing. Any issues can be debugged without a long compile-build-deploy cycle. The packaged app can be delivered to various infrastructures like staging or pre-prod and production using pre-existing deployment solutions.

Application capacity planning is often outside the scope of LCDPs. Organizations often adopt deployment practices, like containers and serverless, to apply scaling measures across the entire ecosystem. Applications developed with LCDPs are no exception to this governance.

Flexibility

Thus, in the absence of a full-fledged programming environment, they must offer a wide range of integrations. These integrations are often provided as pre-built components like plugins and widgets, which can capture and transform data. Some of the pre-built components include the following:

- Location services using GPS on mobile devices

- Cameras, including gesture and facial recognition, etc.

- Audio support, including sound generation and voice recognition

- Multilanguage support

- SQL and NoSQL support for manipulating data

- Log file and audit trail support in applications requiring governance

However, off-the-shelf components might not be enough, so providing a framework to adapt the LCDP for custom integrations is essential. Such integration requires the support of popular data exchange protocols like SOAP, REST, GraphQL, etc.

Cloud-First

LCDPs are primarily offered as software as a service (SAAS). They can be used from the web browser and host the developed applications. The SAAS model frees users from installing the development platform and maintaining infrastructure for deployed applications. It also lowers the entry barrier for new users, who can evaluate such platforms and even develop and deliver small-scale applications at no cost from the familiar environment of their web browser.

Almost all LCDPs can also integrate and deploy the developed applications to the organization's cloud provider. This way, it can enforce the required checks without needing a DevOps team. The integration can dramatically reduce the time and effort required to release applications (and updates) to users.

All the preceding characteristics of LCDPs make them a strategic solution for digital transformations. They can serve as a medium for operation excellency via rapid application development and delivery. However, LCDPs not only provide quick go-to-market solutions but also bridge the software developement supply-chain gap by empowering non-programmer business users, also known as citizen developers, for software development. The platform provides business analysts full autonomy to solve their unique productivity challenges.

Citizen Developers

Humans have always been the force behind all innovations, and as such, technology and tools should never be a barrier. Business analysts and operational teams experience several challenges while servicing their intended customers. When armed with an LCDP and supported by the organization and IT, they become citizen developers. It is important to note that citizen developers may not have any formal training in programming. Moreover, software development may not be their actual job responsibility. But these folks are involved with day-to-day operational challenges and can think of creative ideas to solve them. Consequently, LCDP delivers the ability to develop, adapt, and deploy software quickly, a pivotal factor in business competitiveness. LCDP adoption enthusiasm is additionally fueled by impressive success stories across several organizations; for example:

- T-Mobile US Inc developed its Covid-19 Employee Roster Mobile App using LCDP. Being the third largest wireless carrier in the United States, they provided an essential service. The employee roster app enabled T-Mobile to serve customers when almost all their stores were temporarily closed. The internal application captured real-time information on employee availability and provided insights to field managers. It was developed and deployed within a matter of days in March 2020 by a team of business analysts.

- *Time* magazine, a century-old brand with a huge print and online audience, adopted LCDP for its vendor management process. The internal application was aimed to do away with the repetitive, manual processes in content sourcing, like planning, budgeting, invoicing, payments, etc. The app had several benefits, like reduced payment cycles from months to days and streamlined vendor communication, bringing transparency and efficiency to the content creation processes.

- Heathrow Airport, one of the largest and busiest airports, has empowered all airport front-line employees with an LCDP. These employees have made numerous applications for several challenges across different aspects of airport operations. These apps automated 950 hours of effort and eliminated 75,000 sheets of paperwork, thus yielding impressive cost and time benefits.

It is crucial to note that citizen developers must have an aptitude for using tools to their advantage to find solutions but don't need intensive training. Further, because many are digital natives who grew up with and understand the value of software, they are open to learning and implementing new tools that increase productivity and assist their workflow. The development of administrative and reporting apps, for example, is one area where citizen developers can be of greatest use within enterprise organizations. These applications currently run on spreadsheets or database tools and may include data-tracking and workflow or administrative apps. Moving them to an LCDP allows IT to control all these applications, rather than having dozens of unsynchronized, unmonitored applications in every team.

As discussed previously, low-code tools and techniques have existed since commercial software development began. Their use was limited to developers and IT experts, who accomplished specific objectives in software development to reduce overall effort. Meanwhile, the LCDP democratizes software development for everyone by lowering the entry barrier. Applications built by citizen developers can describe radical business solutions more accurately than any product requirement document. The power of LCDP is that it will allow us to capitalize on human potential to solve problems and transform organizations.

Digital transformation has been an essential agenda item for business leaders. The effects of the pandemic increased the need for digital transformation while revealing the huge worldwide shortage of skilled developers. As a result, citizen development has emerged as a contemporary method of encouraging employees without enterprise IT skills to become software developers, thereby promoting the principle: "Software is everyone's business."

Appsmith Low-code Platform

Appsmith is one of the leading open-source low-code platforms that allows users to develop internal tools and perform workflow automation quickly. The platform offers a range of features and tools, including drag-and-drop UI design, database and API connectors, role-based access control, and workflow automation. Each component is customizable, so users have a lot of flexibility to adapt the components as per requirements without sacrificing speed or efficiency.

Appsmith's open-source license is one of its most significant advantages. It provides several benefits, like no vendor lock-in and self-hosted environments for compliance checks and cost control. Being open source, you can investigate its design, get the list of dependencies, perform security scans and dependency updates, and customize integrations. You also get the opportunity to contribute critical features or any integrations that matter to you. Finally, with open source, you have more control over building, deploying, and securing your data. You can also perform security audits on the codebase to ensure that it meets your InfoSec requirements. Let us have a quick overview of the features of the platform.

Graphical Console

Appsmith provides a graphical console that offers several functions, like application management, release management, user management, etc. The application console has a palette and a canvas interface with which to build a rich UI for each application. The palette provides over 40 widgets, including containers for layout, that can be dragged and dropped on the canvas. All components are responsive, by design, and can automatically resize while maintaining their aspect ratio. Users are required to place the visual component, and the UI automatically adjusts itself to accommodate the new component.

The components available include simple controls, such as text labels, date picker, and input boxes; several types of buttons, like click and radio; fluid containers for layout, lists, and tabs for grouping and forms; and media controls, such as pictures, video players, camera and audio recorder; as well as advanced controls, like code scanner, document viewers, and location maps.

Data Sources

Appsmith provides pre-built connectors to extract data from a wide variety of data stores. These connectors are based on native implementations of each store and provide the capability to load, update, or save data. You are only required to provide the location and credentials to connect to the database. The connection information is stored in an encrypted manner and is used to create connection pools while deploying the app. The list of supported data stores (Table 1-1) includes SQL, NoSQL, file, and data warehouse.

Table 1-1. *Appsmith-supported Databases*

Database Name	Type
MYSQL	SQL
MariaDB	SQL
Postgres	SQL
SQL Server	SQL
Elasticsearch	NoSQL
MongoDB	NoSQL
DynamoDB	NoSQL
Firestore	NoSQL
Snowflake	SQL(Warehouse)

You can create, test, and name queries against each of your data sources. These queries are then used to load data in appropriate widgets, like dropdowns and tables. Additionally, operators can transform the data from one form to another. There are input boxes and data forms to update or insert data. Appsmith is reactive. Thus, the widgets are automatically updated whenever the data in the query changes.

Dataflow

Appsmith offers dataflow controls to enable quick and simplified development of streaming data pipelines. These controls are built around client-side capabilities. Each control can perform several validations before pulling the data. By default, all data is pulled sequentially, as shown in Figure 1-1, but you can improve the concurrency by performing parallel execution of data queries across various data sources, as shown in Figure 1-2.

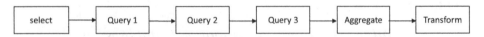

Figure 1-1. *Dataflow composition*

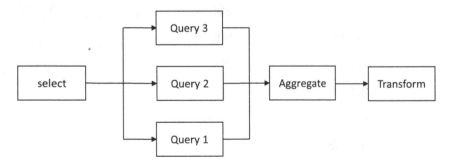

Figure 1-2. *Parallel dataflow*

Imperative programming typically requires using callbacks and synchronization objects, such as locks, to coordinate tasks and access shared data. By using the dataflow functional programming paradigm, you can create dataflow objects that process data as it becomes available. It is a form of declarative programming where the entire data flow is expressed as a composable transformation.

Versioning

Version control offers several benefits, like collaboration, by allowing several people to contribute changes, and experimentation, by allowing one to rollback changes. It is one of the fundamental practices of software development. Application versioning is the foundation for shipping changes at high velocity and desired software quality.

Appsmith does not provide its own version control system. Instead, it integrates with any Git hosting provider. Git providers like GitHub and GitLab are widely used in organizations to enforce several practices, as shown in Figure 1-3, like reviews, quality checks, build failures, etc. Integrating with a provider enforces all these standards for Appsmith applications as well. You can run your app's test suite as part of the continuous integration (CI) workflow and have confidence in any change before merging and deploying it.

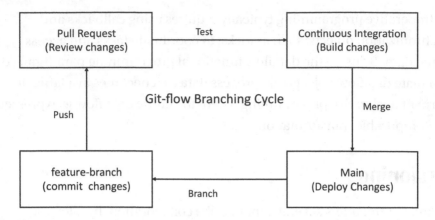

Figure 1-3. *Git support*

Version control also offers traceability and change governance, which are necessary for any development. Developers must be able to track down why and when a change was introduced. When an outage or a bug is reported, a quick lookup of all these details is required to perform the root-cause analysis.

GraphQL and REST Support

Appsmith integrates with several popular tools, like S3, Zapier, Slack, Shopify, Mixpanel, etc. These are REST-based connectors where the integration is accomplished based on platform API. This also means that if you need to integrate an out-of-box unsupported tool, then you can leverage the generic REST connector, as shown in Figure 1-4. The connector can consume data using JavaScript object notation (JSON) format.

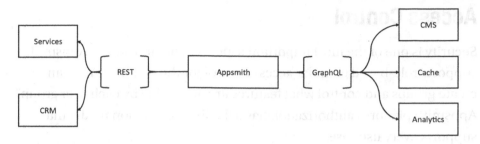

Figure 1-4. *Appsmith-supported API protocols*

Appsmith provides integration with GraphQL, as shown in Figure 1-4, for reading and manipulating data. GraphQL is an open-source query language that lets you fetch and manipulate data from APIs. The protocol provides the flexibility of specifying interested data fields to the user. This promotes an optimized data exchange instead of sending everything over the wire. Often a single query in GraphQL loads data from multiple databases. Since GraphQL is database agnostic, it can be used to integrate any data store. You only need to make sure the respective datastore provides a GraphQL API.

White Labeling

Generated apps often don't match up with your brand. They are built using generic layouts, fonts, and color schemes that differ from your organization's preferences. Moreover, the application logo will never match up to the prescribed guidelines. In summary, generated applications do not feel like they are a part of the organization landscape.

Appsmith provides capabilities to modify and control the appearance of your apps with custom styles. You can either rework the styling in every app you make or create templates that can be reused to enforce the same styles. Often, consistency in your application's UI components is quite vital. It allows your customers to navigate your app easily. They can find what they are looking for without thinking about it, creating a great user experience.

Access Control

Security is one of the most important aspects of organizations. Appsmith supports role-based granular access control for the platform. You can create groups and control what features are accessible by each user group. Appsmith platform authorization has a flexible permission model that supports every use case.

Applications developed using Appsmith can perform user authentication using JSON web tokens (JWT). Users can provide their credentials, which a server-side application will verify, and a valid JWT token is returned. Managing application user credentials is outside the scope of the platform.

However, in enterprises, we do not want to have the risk that comes with managing multiple accounts for every user. This makes the management of access control a difficult task. Appsmith also supports single sign-on (SSO) with SAML, as shown in Figure 1-5, thus eliminating the need for a credentials exchange. Users only need to sign in one time, against an identity provider, to access multiple service providers. This allows for a faster authentication process and fewer expectations that the user must remember multiple login credentials for every application for which SAML transfers the identity information to the service providers. This form of authentication ensures that credentials are only sent to the identity provider directly.

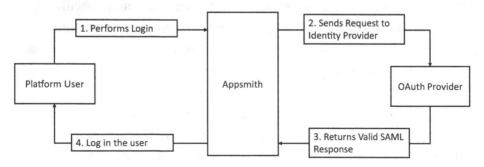

Figure 1-5. *SSO handshake*

SOC Compliant

Organizations using cloud platforms are continuously exposed to security and data risks arising out of third-party software usage. These risks can materialize in several ways, like leaked user credentials/keys, exposed business sensitivity, vulnerabilities in deployed applications, etc. This can result in serious financial, legal, and reputational impacts and may threaten the organization's survival. Hence, evaluating the risk before adopting a cloud platform is imperative.

Appsmith is certified by System and Organization Controls (SOC) and can be safely trusted with your organization's data. SOC is a security framework that specifies how cloud service providers should protect customer data from unauthorized access, security incidents, and other vulnerabilities. Often a third-party audit is performed to validate that the applied controls, as shown in Figure 1-6, are as per the specification. The resultant certification and report demonstrate how the Appsmith cloud platform achieves key security policies and objectives.

Figure 1-6. *SOC practices*

Limitations

Appsmith is instrumental to developing applications that leverage its capabilities. If a feature is available, then it can be used with ease. But some solutions can demand features that are well beyond the current capabilities of Appsmith. In these scenarios, Appsmith can pose major challenges to operate and thus may not be a product fit. In the following sections, let's look at some of the use cases that should be avoided with Appsmith.

Customer-engaged Applications

Often user engagement is one of the key metrics businesses are interested in. Marketing teams would frequently track, analyze, and update application interfaces to optimize engagement. Organizations often aim to get higher engagement as it translates to customer loyalty.

At first, Appsmith can seem to be an appropriate fit for quickly developing the customer interface. However, the overall solution would be difficult to manage and update iteratively. Appsmith is well designed to pull data from various sources, transform it, and show it using various components. These components can be styled using templates. These templates are suitable for controlling the coloring scheme, font, size, etc. But it can be challenging to perform several common operations, such as the following:

- Control the grid position
- Layer component buttons and data form for animations
- Perform interactive drag-drop operations
- Do push notifications
- Add chatbots

All these tasks are required to constructively engage the user at multiple touchpoints for their benefit.

Enterprise Integration

In the modern enterprise, all systems across the entire business ecosystem must work together as a well-oiled machine. These systems must share data in real time to deliver new customer experiences and services. Enterprise integration eases the flow of data within complex information and operating systems by providing a middleware layer to act as a common interface between each separate application, system, and service.

Appsmith can readily consume data from various data sources or over APIs. But there is limited capacity to push data for enterprise collaboration, a.k.a, event passing. Event delivery is often accomplished by using diverse technologies like SOAP, web services, JSON, RPC, GraphQL, multicast, unicast, etc. Due to the limited scope of programming, it is challenging to extend Appsmith for unsupported middleware tools. In such cases, it is often prudent to build Appsmith applications for data capture only. Data can be sent to middleware using custom scripts or third-party tools.

Complex Business Process

An organization runs several processes during all day-to-day activities. The majority of these services can be straightforward, like loading data, validating details, and so on. But a few of them can be composed of several steps, like generating snapshots, aggregating data, capturing metrics, performing notifications, etc. Additionally, these steps can be performed in either a recurring or scheduled manner, making the overall solution quite complex.

Appsmith can be readily used to aggregate data across various sources. It can generate projections for insights and analytics. But it would need workarounds to perform scheduled/recurring executions, create snapshots, deliver event notifications, and other tasks. Thus, an application that requires these capabilities must be designed outside Appsmith.

Appsmith Setup

Appsmith is released quite often. The Appsmith open-source repository [https://github.com/appsmithorg/appsmith/releases] lists source artifacts and release notes for every release. When this book was written, Appsmith 1.9.16, as shown in Figure 1-7, was the latest version.

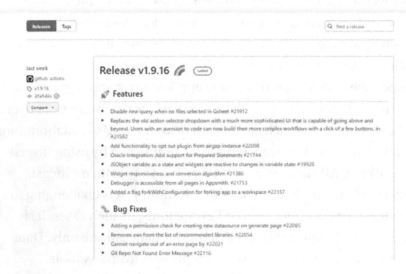

Figure 1-7. *Appsmith releases*

Appsmith is not released as a binary package, because it is difficult to support various chip architectures. Instead, container images of every release are made available in the Docker-Hub registry.

You need to install Docker Desktop to deploy Appsmith on your workstation. Installation of Docker Desktop is beyond the scope of this book. Please refer to the steps mentioned on https://www. docker.com/products/docker-desktop/.

As a prerequisite, let's check if Docker is set up correctly by executing the following command:

```
$ docker version
Client:
 Cloud integration: v1.0.31
 Version:           20.10.24
 API version:       1.41
 Go version:        go1.19.7
 Git commit:        297e128
 Built:             Tue Apr  4 18:28:08 2023
#
# Output Bridged for Brevity
```

Please make sure you have an account on Docker-Hub so that you can access the available container images. You can log in to your account either from the CLI by using the docker login command as shown here, or from the Docker Desktop admin console.

```
$ docker login
Log in with your Docker ID to push and pull images from Docker-
Hub. If you don't have a Docker ID, head over to https://hub.
docker.com to create one.
Username: docker_username
Password: docker_password
```

Create a folder named stacks. It will be used to persist Appsmith data to avoid data loss when the container restarts. You can then use the docker run command to download and start the Appsmith container, as shown here:

```
$ docker run -it -p 80:80 -v ./stacks:/appsmith-stacks
appsmith/appsmith-ce
Unable to find image 'appsmith/appsmith-ce:latest' locally
```

```
latest: Pulling from appsmith/appsmith-ce
Digest: sha256:fe11195852bcade42a38a3bd751d862f47793d2
4d2319053758cc9f4180cfc81
Status: Downloaded newer image for appsmith/appsmith-ce:latest
#
# Output Bridged for Brevity
```

The preceding command has parameters that configure Appsmith as follows:

- Download the latest released version of appsmith/appsmith-ce.

- Bind container port 80 to the port 80 of the host. This will make sure you can access Appsmith using http://localhost.

- Bind a directory named stacks to the container directory app smith-stacks. This will persist all generated applications and configurations on the host disk so that you do not lose work if Appsmith is restarted.

- Run the container in interactive mode to make all logs available on your console.

Alternatively, Appsmith documentation also provides container specification in YAML format. You can download the file to run the docker container, as previously specified.

```
$ curl -L https://bit.ly/docker-compose-CE -o $PWD/docker-compose.yml
```

Download the Appsmith container using the docker-compose command:

```
$ docker-compose up
[+] Running 2/2
 ✓ Network home_default   Created      0.5s
 ✓ Container appsmith     Created      1.7s
Attaching to appsmith
#
# Output Bridged for Brevity
```

Access Appsmith Console

Appsmith Console is a web application that can be accessed using your favorite browser. Both of the preceding commands start Appsmith on HTTP port 80. Thus, you should be able to access it using the http:// localhost web URL, as shown in Figure 1-8. The web page should show a welcome message with a Get Started call to action (CTA).

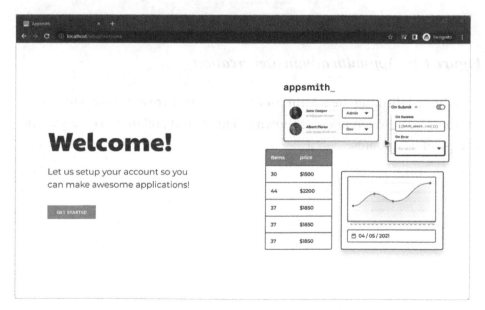

Figure 1-8. *Appsmith landing UI*

Once you click the Get Started button, you are presented with a form to create admin user details, as shown in Figure 1-9. The user will be allowed to perform all actions. In Chapter 7, you will look at how to configure groups and roles while onboarding users to the platform.

Figure 1-9. *Appsmith admin user creation*

After confirming the admin user creation, you are at the last step. It captures your preferences, as shown in Figure 1-10, related to data sharing and product updates.

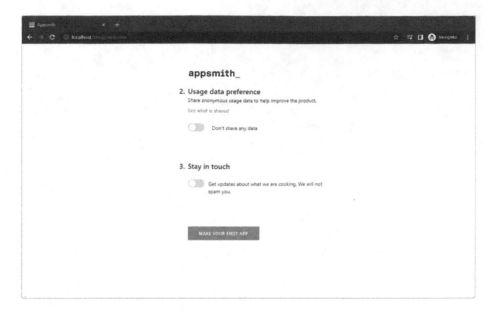

Figure 1-10. *User preferences*

You are ready to use Appsmith now. It presents the console, as shown in Figure 1-11, to create applications, templates, configure settings, etc. You will learn all these features in upcoming chapters.

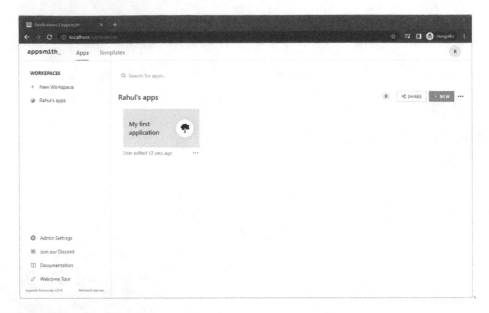

Figure 1-11. User login console

Appsmith Editions

You deployed the Appsmith community edition on your workstation in the previous section. The community edition is free and good enough to experience Appsmith. It is shipped without several enterprise-specific features, warranty, and support, though. Let's have a quick look at the various editions provided by Appsmith:

- **Community Edition:** The Appsmith cloud edition runs on the community edition. It can be installed on your infrastructure as well. It offers all the app development features, including all UI widgets and data sources. However, user signup is limited to social platforms. There is no SAML integration for enterprise user onboarding. Also, there are limited roles to enforce user privileges. It is important to note that this is free of any charge and is without any formal warranty or support.

- **Business Edition:** This edition must be installed on your infrastructure. It is licensed on a per-user basis and goes beyond the community edition. It offers SSO login integration with a wide variety of OAuth providers. There is white labeling support to apply your organization's UI guidelines. You get audit logs support and granular access controls for enforcing user privileges across the platform features.

The book will primarily work with the community edition, as all application development features are readily available. If the business edition is required, the section would mention that wherever applicable.

Summary

Low-code development has always been there in different forms, like CASE tools, RAD tools, and fourth-generation languages. Over the past decade, it has gained a lot of focus. It lowers the barrier to entry for innovation. People with no formal coding experience can build digital solutions for their challenges. While there are immediate benefits of an LCDP, it also has limitations. Appsmith is an open-source LCDP and offers several features. Each of these features will be discussed in detail in subsequent chapters. The chapter also provides hands-on instructions for downloading and starting Appsmith on a workstation. You are able to access the Appsmith Console in your browser and start developing your first application!

CHAPTER 2

Working with the Canvas Editor

In the previous chapter, we walked through how to install Appsmith on your local environment using a Docker image. Now that you have it up and running, it's time to dive into the platform and build some applications!

In this chapter, you will explore the various features of Appsmith and learn how to use them to build robust applications. You will start by looking at the Appsmith Canvas Editor, where you will spend most of your time building your applications. The editor is a drag-and-drop interface where you can quickly add widgets, data sources, and custom code to your application.

You will also explore the Appsmith Dashboard—the central hub for managing your applications, databases, and API connections. The dashboard lists all the apps you have created using Appsmith, allows you to create new workspaces to organize them, and also lets you access admin settings and documentation.

The Dashboard and the Canvas Editor will give you a solid foundation to start your low-code application development journey. By the end of this chapter, you will be able to create a sample application to whet your appetite, which will also pave the way toward building more complex applications, with data connectivity, later in the book.

© Rahul Sharma and Rajat Arora 2023
R. Sharma and R. Arora, *Low-Code Development with Appsmith*,
https://doi.org/10.1007/978-1-4842-9813-8_2

Running Appsmith for the First Time

We already installed Appsmith using its Docker image in Chapter 1. It is time to run it for the first time and familiarize ourselves with its various elements. To begin, please ensure that Appsmith's Docker container is still running, and navigate to `http://localhost` with your favorite web browser. You should be able to see a screen like the one shown in Figure 2-1 (yes, complete with virtual confetti!).

Figure 2-1. *The Appsmith Welcome screen*

Go ahead and click on the "Get Started" button. You will be redirected to a form to create an account and answer a couple of questions. Fill in the details and click on "Next." The next screen will ask for your telemetry and communication preferences. Feel free to opt out and click the "Make your first app" button.

You will be presented with a Welcome screen explaining various features of Appsmith in a nutshell (Figure 2-2). All of these will be covered in this book's following chapters. Click the "Build on My Own" button (or close the screen with the close icon on the top right corner) to enter the Canvas Editor.

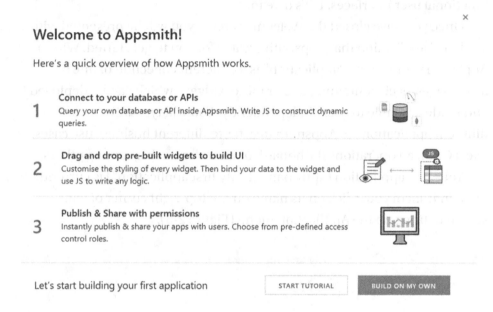

Figure 2-2. *Almost there, to the Canvas Editor!*

Introducing the Canvas Editor

The Canvas Editor is the centerpiece of Appsmith's low-code platform. It helps you create elegant user interfaces (UIs) by dragging and dropping various UI elements into it, using a large number of configurable widgets like input boxes, buttons, forms, tables, charts, and so on. You can create any kind of application UI by arranging these widgets on the Canvas Editor, and later on add interactive functionality to your application by configuring them. The Canvas Editor's flexibility and adaptability make it an ideal solution for businesses and individual developers looking to build custom applications quickly and efficiently.

In this chapter, we will focus on the various features of the Canvas Editor and look at some different widgets it offers you to create beautiful, functional user interfaces. Let's dive in!

Once you have closed the Welcome screen, you will be presented with a "blank" application that Appsmith creates for you to get started. Within Appsmith's context, an "application" is a coherent collection of one or more pages, each containing one or more widgets, which can be deployed and made available to users independently. You will typically create different applications in Appsmith to cater to different business use cases, like a CRM, an operations dashboard, or an order tracker, among others.

Your first application (aptly named "My first application") is currently open in front of you. Click on its name on the top-right corner of your screen to bring up the Application menu (Figure 2-3).

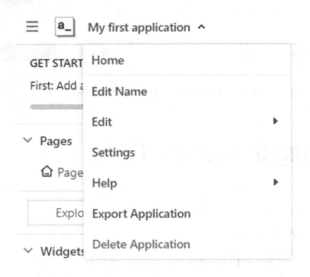

Figure 2-3. *Application menu*

If you want, you can change the application's name to something to your liking by using the "Edit Name" option. The Application menu gives you a lot of other options too, as follows:

- Access Appsmith's documentation, community forums, Discord channel, and GitHub repository using the "Help" option.

- Export your application (as a JSON file) using the "Export Application" option. This JSON file can be later imported into Appsmith.

- Undo / Redo your actions on the Canvas Editor using the "Edit" option.

- Delete your application using the "Delete Application" option.

Caution   Once deleted, applications cannot be restored within Appsmith. Make sure you create a backup using the "Export Application" option before deleting an application.

Application Settings

The "Settings" option in the application menu opens a sidebar to the right, where you can edit different settings for your application (Figure 2-4).

Figure 2-4. *The application settings sidebar*

The **General** tab lets you change your application's name, as well as choose an icon for it. The icon will be displayed alongside your application in the Appsmith Dashboard.[1]

The **Share & Embed** tab allows you to share your application with different users and to make your application public. Public applications can also be embedded inside different web applications. We will revisit these concepts (along with a larger discussion on access controls) in Chapter 6.

With the **Theme** tab, you can control the overall appearance of your application. Themes control the various fonts and colors displayed in your application, as well as default values for border radius and box shadows.

You can either select one of the many predefined themes available, or design your own by selecting individual values for App Font, Primary and

---

[1] You will take a look at the Appsmith Dashboard in later sections of this chapter.

Secondary Colors, Border Radius, and Box Shadow. Values selected here will apply to all widgets you use in your application, and you will also have the option to change these values for individual widgets.

The **Navigation** tab lets you define the properties of the navigation bar in the deployed version of your application. You can select its position (Top or Side), color (Light or the theme's primary color), and whether you want to show the "Sign In" button for logged-out users.[2]

Finally, the **Page Settings** section displays the different pages in your application and allows you to change their properties, like Page Name, URL, Navigation Bar visibility, and Home Page configuration.

Your application will only have one page at this point of time. As we move on to develop complex applications in further chapters, we will add more pages here and learn how to navigate among them.

Application Components

Once you close the Settings sidebar (by clicking the » icon on its top left corner), you will notice that another sidebar has appeared on the left side of your screen.[3] See Figure 2-5.

---

[2] There is a nuance here. If your app is private, your users will have to log in before accessing it. For public apps, this setting will allow your users to optionally sign in if they already have an account;, otherwise, they can continue using your app as anonymous users.

[3] It was already there, but the appearance of the Settings sidebar caused it to close.

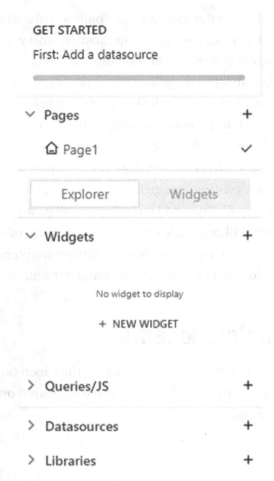

Figure 2-5. *The left-hand sidebar*

This sidebar lists each and every component of your application. The first section shows the different pages your application has. The other sections list the widgets, queries, data sources, and libraries you have added to your applications.

Widgets are the UI elements, like forms, text boxes, and buttons, that you can drag and drop on the Canvas Editor.

Data sources contain connections to different sources of data, like databases (SQL and NoSQL), APIs (REST/Graphql), and even products like Google Sheets and Airtable.

Queries/JS contain references to any custom JavaScript (JS) snippets you have written in the application and queries against any added data sources.

Libraries contain references to any external JS libraries you require in your application. Appsmith includes popular libraries like lodash, moment, xmlParser, and forge by default.

You will get to know more about data sources, queries, JS, and libraries in Chapters 3 and 4. For now, let's look at all the widgets available in Appsmith for you to use in your low-code applications.

Click on the Widgets tab on the left-hand sidebar, next to the Explorer tab, to bring up the list. At the time of publication of this book, there were 45 different widgets available (Figure 2-6).

Figure 2-6. *Some of the different widgets available in Appsmith*

These widgets range from simple input widgets, like **Input**, **Phone Input**, **Currency Input**, and **Checkbox**; advanced input widgets, like **Multi-Select**, **File Picker**, and **Range Slider**; form widgets, like **Form** and **JSON Form**; display widgets, like **Table**, **Chart**, **Map**, and **Progress**; and even state-of-the-art widgets, like **Audio Recorder**, **Camera**, and **QR Code Scanner**. With such a wide range of widgets available, Appsmith has made sure that no use case gets ignored while you are creating low-code applications.

The Greetings Application

To help you better understand how Appsmith works, without distracting you with features and concepts that you haven't been introduced to yet, let's create a small greetings application. This application will have you input your name inside an input box, and when you click on a specified button, a notification will appear on screen with your name on it.

Using Appsmith, you can create this *without* writing a single line of code, and this will also whet your appetite for more complex topics detailed later in the book.

In the following sections, we will introduce three different widgets, namely the Text widget, the Input widget, and the Button widget. At the end of each section we will bring you one step closer to building the toy application we described.

Text Widget

The Text widget is one of the simplest Appsmith widgets to work with. It is used to display some text on your application. The text can either be static—for example, displaying the name of your application in a heading—or be referenced from a data source or a JavaScript snippet.

Appsmith allows you to configure the widget in a variety of ways, including its dimensions, styling, visibility, animations, and so on. You will notice that most of these options are also available to other Appsmith widgets.

Let us drag our first widget onto the Canvas Editor, shall we? Open the list of widgets on the left-hand sidebar, scroll down to the bottom and locate the Text widget, drag it out, and place it anywhere on the Canvas Editor. As soon as you do that, you will find that your screen has transformed.

First, there is a widget visible on the screen (Figure 2-7).

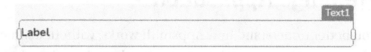

Figure 2-7. *The Text widget*

In addition, you will notice that another sidebar has appeared on the right side of the screen (Figure 2-8).

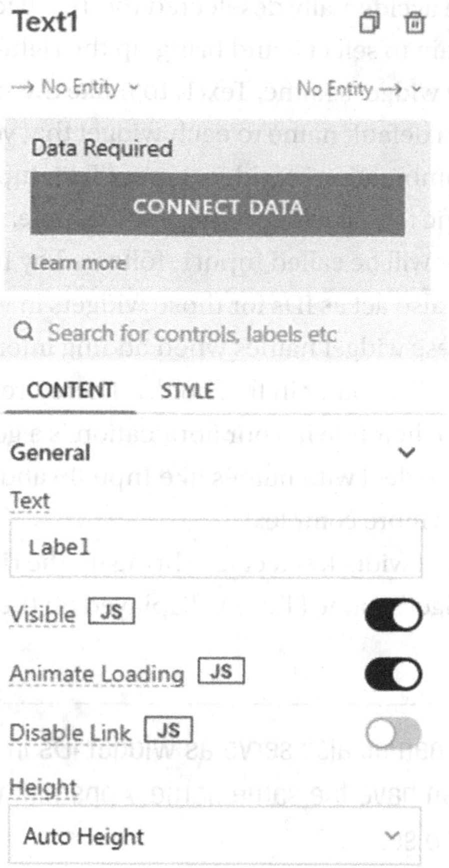

Text1

⤏ No Entity ⌄   No Entity ⤏ ⌄

Data Required

CONNECT DATA

Learn more

🔍 Search for controls, labels etc

CONTENT   STYLE

General   ⌄

Text

Label

Visible JS   ⬤

Animate Loading JS   ⬤

Disable Link JS   ○

Height

Auto Height   ⌄

Figure 2-8. *The right-hand sidebar*

As opposed to the left-hand sidebar, which represents the entire application, the right-hand sidebar represents a single widget. It allows you to control and update various properties of the currently selected widget. As different widgets have different properties, you will find that the structure of the right-hand sidebar can change drastically from widget to widget.

In case you have accidentally deselected the Text widget in the Canvas Editor, click on it again to select it and bring up the right-hand sidebar. You can also click on the widget's name, Text1, to make the sidebar appear.

Appsmith gives a default name to each widget that you drag out on the Canvas Editor—a combination of widget types (Text, Input, Select, etc.) and a counter specific to that widget type. For example, the first input box on the Canvas Editor will be called Input1, followed by Input2, Input3, and so on. These names also act as IDs for those widgets in your application. You must refer to these widget names when adding interactivity or binding data to them (as we will do later in this book). Therefore, renaming these widgets according to their role in your application is a good practice. After all, you do not want to deal with names like Input49 and Button55 as your application becomes more complex!

To rename the text widget, select it to bring up the right-hand sidebar and click on the widget's name (Text1), displayed on the sidebar's top left corner.

Note   As widget names also serve as widget IDs in your application, no two widgets can have the same name. Appsmith will raise an error if you attempt to do so.

The right-hand sidebar also lets you control other aspects of the text widget. For example, to change the text displayed by the widget, look for a property called Text in the General section of the Content tab. There are a few more properties you can modify in the Content tab, as shown in Table 2-1.

Table 2-1. *Widget Content Properties*

Property	Meaning	Default Value
Visible	Changes the visibility of the widget. Makes the widget translucent in the Canvas Editor and turns off its visibility completely in the published app.	True
Animate Loading	Controls the animation while loading the widget in the published app.	True
Disable Link	When enabled, turns off link parsing for text inside Text property.	False

Using the Height property, you can also control how the widget's height responds to the content (specified with the Text property). The following configurations are possible:

- **Auto Height (default)**: The widget's height will expand or contract as per the content displayed. You cannot specify the widget's height with this option selected.

- **Fixed**: This option allows you to set the widget's height in the Canvas Editor. If the content is larger than the widget's size, the widget will cut it off.

- **Auto Height with limits**: The widget's height will expand or contract as per the content displayed, *subject to a maximum and a minimum*. Once you select this option, you will notice *two* anchors for controlling the widget's height on the Canvas Editor. The first anchor will control the widget's minimum height, and the second the maximum. The widget's maximum height has to be *at least* one row more than its minimum height. The widget will cut off the content if it exceeds its maximum size.

Controlling a Widget's Look and Feel

Appsmith also allows you to control a widget's look and feel. You can change its font, color, and size, apply borders, make the text bold or italic, and change its alignment. You can control these settings in the Style tab on the right-hand sidebar.

The Style tab gives the following options for a Text widget:

- **Font Family**: This allows you to change the font of the displayed text. You can choose from a list of ten predefined fonts (with popular fonts like Open Sans, Nunito, and Inter being available[4]).

- **Font Size**: Here, you can choose from among a list of six predefined sizes for the displayed text, starting from Small (0.875rem) to 3XL (3.75rem).

- **Text, Background, and Border Colors**: These options are self-explanatory. They let you change the color of the text and the widget's background and border, respectively. You can choose from one of the numerous predefined colors or specify a custom hex code.

- **Text Formatting**: In this section, you can change the horizontal alignment of the displayed text ("center" being the default), and make the text either **bold** or *italic*.

---

[4] You can also bring your own fonts, as you will see in Chapter 4.

- **Border Width**: This lets you control the widget's border width in pixels. You can only specify a numeric value in the input box.[5] The default border width for every widget is zero. The value of the Border Color property will not have any effect unless you provide a positive value for the Border Width property.

For the Greetings Application

For the Greetings application, create a new Text widget and rename it to **Title**. Have the text "Greetings!" display on the widget, and make the text large, bold, and centered. Place the widget center-top on the Canvas Editor. Delete any other widget that may be present on the Canvas Editor at this point. To do that, select the unnecessary widget and press the Delete key on your keyboard.

Input Widget

Appsmith's Input widget is an essential tool for creating web applications with dynamic user interfaces (Figure 2-9). This widget allows users to input data, which can be utilized by the application to interact with databases, APIs, or other services. The Input widget offers a range of features and configuration options, making it a powerful and customizable component in any Appsmith project.

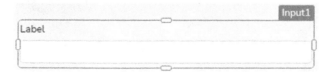

Figure 2-9. *The Input widget*

---

[5] This is not exactly true. In later chapters, you will learn how to specify property values using JavaScript.

One of the key features of the Input widget is its support for different input types. Depending on the data you want to collect, you can choose from text, email, password, number, currency, and telephone[6] input types. This flexibility ensures you can collect and validate data effectively, improving the overall user experience.

Just like the Text widget, the Input widget allows for advanced customization, enabling you to tailor the appearance and behavior of the input field to your specific needs. You can easily modify the placeholder text, which serves as a helpful prompt for users, and set default values to streamline the data-entry process. Additionally, you can adjust the width and height of the input field and apply custom CSS styles to seamlessly integrate the widget into your application's design.

Let's see the Input widget in action now, shall we? Drag the widget from the left-hand sidebar to anywhere on the Canvas Editor. With the widget still selected, take a look at the options that the right-hand sidebar gives you. You will notice that a few more sections have been added in the Content tab.

Data Section

The Data section lets you control the data type of the text expected inside the input box, as well as the default value of the text (Figure 2-10).

---

[6] Currency and Phone Number inputs have different widgets—"Currency Input" and "Phone Input," respectively. Readers are encouraged to explore them along the lines of the Input widget.

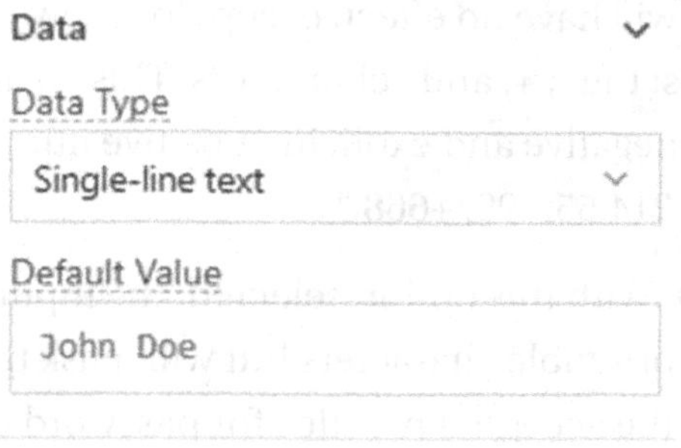

Data   ⌄

Data Type

Single-line text   ⌄

Default Value

John Doe

Figure 2-10. *The Data section*

You can select from a variety of data types for your input widget, as follows:

- **Single-line Text (default)**: The input box will accept all printable characters and will display them in a single line. If the entered text is longer than the width of the Input box, text will scroll toward the left.

- **Multi-line Text**: The input box will accept all printable characters and will display them across multiple lines. If the entered text is longer than the width of the input box, the text will wrap to the following line, making the height of the input box larger.[7] With default settings, this option will also make the height of the input box span at least two lines.

- **Number**: The input box will only accept numeric characters with this option selected and will display them in a single line. Typing any non-numeric

---

[7] This is true if "Auto Height" is enabled for the widget.

character will have no effect, except for a few
exceptions: the -, +, and . characters. This ensures you
can enter negative and explicitly positive numbers and
decimals: 214.55, -99, +668.[8]

- **Password**: With this option selected, the input box will
  accept all printable characters but will mask them with
  dots, as is the accepted practice for password input. A
  small eye icon will also appear on the right-hand side
  of the input box; clicking on it will toggle the masking
  behavior.

- **Email**: The input box will only accept valid[9] email
  addresses.

You can also specify the default value of the widget in the Data section.
This value will be displayed initially when the user loads your app for the
first time. The default value must be the same type as the currently selected
Data Type of the widget; otherwise, Appsmith will display an error.

Label Section

You can modify the label attached to the input field in the Label section
(Figure 2-11).

---

[8] The input box will still complain if you enter an invalid input with allowed
characters, like 345+99.

[9] The input validation is performed via regex to ensure the correct email address.
The widget cannot validate whether the address exists or not.

Figure 2-11. *The Label section*

The Text option allows you to change the label text, with the default value simply being Label. The Position section allows you to change where the label is displayed relative to the input box. You have the following three options:

- **Auto (default)**: This option lets Appsmith decide the optimum position of the label.

- **Top**: This will display the label on top of the input box.

- **Left**: This option will display the label to the left of the input box. This will make the width of the input box smaller as it adjusts to accommodate the label. With this option selected, you will also notice two more options pop up in the current section:

  - **Alignment**: To control the text alignment of the label text, with options being Left (default) and Right.

- **Width (in columns)**: To specify how many columns are given to the label, leaving the rest for the input box. You can specify any numeric value here, subject to the following caveats:

  - The input box has to be at least five columns wide. If you specify a value x, where (`widget-width`) − x < 5, the input box will stop shrinking further.

  - If you specify zero, Appsmith will auto-select an optimum width for the label.

  - If the label text cannot fit within the specified width, it will wrap around in multiple rows (subject to a minimum width of one character, after which the text becomes truncated).

Validation Section

The Validation section enables you to define the rules for an acceptable value to be provided by the user. Some of the properties listed here are global, while the rest show up only when a specific data type is selected (Figure 2-12).

Validation ⌄

Required JS ◯

Max Characters

255

Regex

^\w+@[a-zA-Z_]+?\.[a-zA-Z]

Valid

{{ Input1.text.length > 0 }}

Error Message

Not a valid value!

Spellcheck ◯

Figure 2-12. *The Validation section*

Global Validations

The following properties are available for all data types:

- **Required**: Specifies whether an input is required to be entered by the user or not. Defaults to false.

- **Regex**: Compares the input value to a particular regular expression. An error is displayed if the input does not match the regex.

- **Valid**: Lets you specify a JavaScript expression to test the input value against. The input is considered valid if the JavaScript expression evaluates to true.

- **Error Message**: Here you can specify the error message displayed to the user if the input is invalid. Defaults to Invalid input.

- **Spellcheck**: Determines whether spellchecking is to be performed for user input. A misspelled input is not considered invalid.[10]

Data Type-Specific Validations

There are specific validations available only for Numeric and Text data types:

- **Max Characters** *(Single-line/Multi-line text)*: The maximum number of characters the user can input. Additional keystrokes cease to have any effect once the limit is reached.

- **Min** and **Max** *(Number)*: The minimum and maximum numeric values the user can input.

Regex vs. Valid

Having both Regex and Valid fields available for input validation inside Appsmith, it naturally begs the question: When should you use which method, and are these two methods mutually exclusive? Right off the bat, the answer to the second question is no. We can certainly have situations where either of these may be required.

A regular expression can be used to validate a user's input against a set of predefined rules. For example, as a sample use case, you might want to accept all alphanumeric characters from the user except the digit 8.

---

[10] At the time of publishing this book, spellcheck only reliably works in the Firefox browser. Appsmith uses Mozilla's spellcheck API under the hood.

For this, you can simply validate the input against the following regular expression:

```
^[A-Za-z0-79]*$
```

There is no need to write a JavaScript function for it in the Valid section. If, however, you want to ensure that a password input does not contain easy-to-guess strings, you might have to write a JavaScript function like this in the Valid section:

```
{{
    !["password", "123456", "admin", "qwerty"]
    .some(subStr => {
        return PasswordInput.text.toLowerCase()
        .includes(subStr)
    })
}}
```

Since this is a standard JavaScript code block, we can also make an AJAX call to a server somewhere that can validate the input for us. We will revisit these techniques in further chapters.

General Section

The General section of an Input widget is very similar to the one for the Text widget (Figure 2-13). You can control visibility, loading animation, and height using the same properties available for the Text widget.

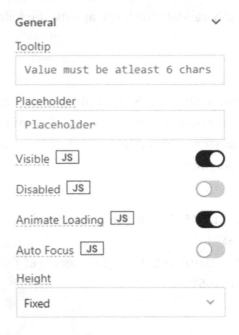

Figure 2-13. *The General section*

A few more properties find their way into the section, though:

- **Disabled**: If set to true, the widget is greyed out and the user cannot input anything into the text box. It defaults to false.

- **Tooltip**: This option provides a way for you to give some description/help-text for the user to help them input the correct information. If set, a small icon appears next to the widget's label, which displays the text when the user hovers their mouse over it.

- **Placeholder**: Here you can mention the placeholder text that gets displayed whenever the input box is empty.

- **Auto Focus**: When selected, the widget will have focus automatically on the published app.

There is another section, Events, below the General section, that lets you stipulate certain actions in the app when certain events related to the widget occur. Since this section is JavaScript heavy, we will revisit it in Chapter 4.

For the Greetings Application

For the Greetings application, create a new Input widget and rename it to **Name**. Set its data type to be "Single-line Text," its label to "Your Name," displayed to the left of the input box, and set a validation to not accept text of more than 100 characters. Configure the text "Please enter your full name" as a tooltip.

Move the widget just below the **Title** widget and remove any unnecessary widgets from the Canvas Editor.

The Button Widget

The Button widget is a powerful tool that can be used to create interactive and engaging user interfaces. It can be used to perform a variety of actions, such as navigating between pages, submitting forms, opening modals, and executing queries. The Button widget is also highly customizable, allowing users to change its appearance, behavior, and functionality to suit their specific needs.

The Button widget is a great way to improve the usability of your app. By adding buttons to your app, you can make it easier for users to perform the actions they need to do. For example, you could add a button to submit a form, open a modal, or execute a query. Buttons can also be used to add visual interest to your app. By using different button styles and colors, you can create a more visually appealing and engaging user interface.

53

The Button widget is a versatile tool that can be used to create a variety of different user interfaces. To see the Button widget in action, drag it out from the left sidebar and place it anywhere on the Canvas Editor. Its default avatar looks like Figure 2-14.

Figure 2-14. *The Button widget*

On the styling front, you can control the text shown on the button, its color and dimensions, its variant (primary, secondary, or tertiary), its icon, and its placement, along with the button text.

When you select the Button widget on the Canvas Editor, its right sidebar looks like Figure 2-15.

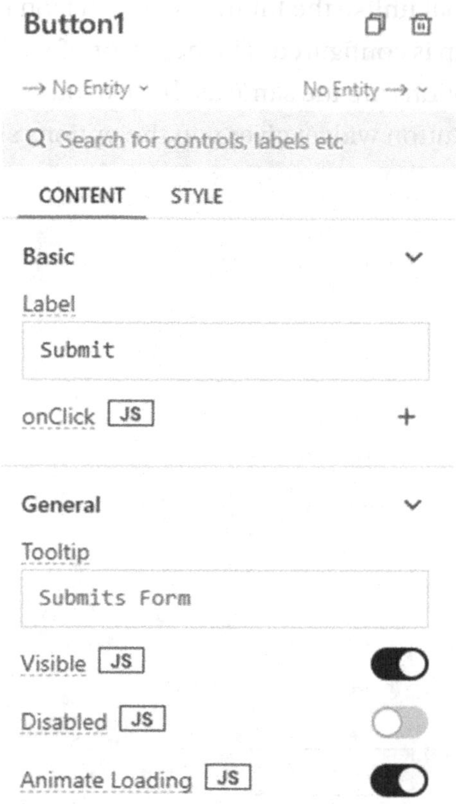

Button1   ⬚ 🗑

→ No Entity ⌄   No Entity → ⌄

🔍 Search for controls, labels etc

CONTENT   STYLE

Basic   ⌄

Label

> Submit

onClick JS   +

General   ⌄

Tooltip

> Submits Form

Visible JS   ⬤

Disabled JS   ◯

Animate Loading JS   ⬤

Figure 2-15. Button widget's configuration

You will notice that most of the options are similar to those offered by the Text and Input widgets. The **Label** option controls the text shown on the button, the **Tooltip** option, when set, shows a tooltip when the user hovers their mouse pointer over the button. The tooltip shown is slightly different from the one shown by the Input widget though (Figure 2-16).

Figure 2-16. Tooltips on the Button widget

You will notice that unlike the Input widget, an icon is not shown next to the label if a tooltip is configured. The behavior of Visible, Disabled, and Animate Loading options are the same as those of other Appsmith widgets.

For styling, the Button widget gives you the options shown in Figure 2-17.

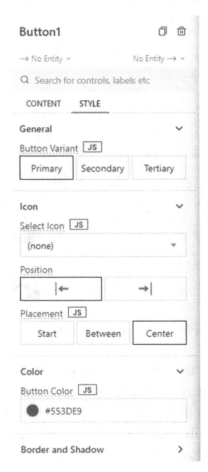

Figure 2-17. *Button widget's style configuration*

You can configure three different variants for the Button widget, namely, primary, secondary, and tertiary, with each variant being less conspicuous than the previous one (Figure 2-18). The widget is created with the primary configuration as the default.

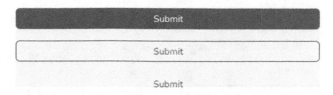

Figure 2-18. *Primary, secondary, and tertiary buttons*

You can also choose an icon to be displayed next to the button's label, using the "Select Icon" option (Figure 2-19).

Figure 2-19. *Button widget with icon*

By default, the icon is displayed to the left of the label, but you can control this by using the **Position** option. Similarly, the **Placement** option controls the relative position of both the icon and the label. Start positions them to the left, Between positions them in two opposite corners, while the default Center option positions them at the center of the button.

Note   Appsmith uses icons from the Blueprint library. You can see the list of all available icons here: `https://blueprintjs.com/docs/#icons`

Controlling a Button's Behavior

Controlling a button's behavior is the most powerful feature of the Button widget. You can access these options by clicking on the + icon next to "onClick" in the Content section of the Button widget's right-hand sidebar (Figure 2-20).

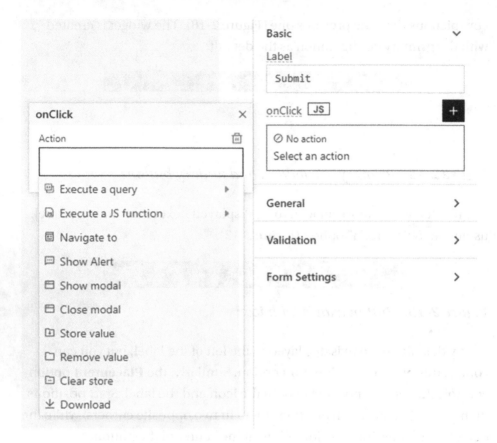

Figure 2-20. *onClick options on the Button widget*

Table 2-2 describes the various actions that the Button widget can perform when the user clicks it.

Table 2-2. *Possible onClick Actions on a Button Widget*

Action	Description
Execute a query	Execute a query against a data source. Data sources and queries are discussed in Chapter 3.
Execute a JS function	Execute a piece of arbitrary JavaScript code. JS code blocks are discussed in Chapter 4.
Navigate to	Navigate to a different page in your application. Requires more than one page to be set up.
Show alert	Show an alert at the top of the page. You can choose between Error, Info, Success, and Warning alert types.
Show / Close Modal	Show or Close a modal window. Requires a widget of type Modal already present on the Canvas Editor.
Store / Remove value	Store or remove a value from a variable.
Clear store	Clear values of all stored variables.
Download	Download some data as a CSV / HTML / Plain Text, or other format file.

Multiple Actions on a Button

You can configure multiple actions with a single button click. For example, you may set up your button to store a value, as well as display an alert, by configuring two actions with its onClick handler (Figure 2-21). These two actions will be executed *at the same time*.

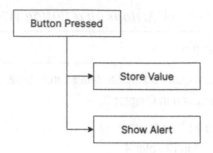

Figure 2-21. *Multiple actions on a button*

That is, you won't be able to access the value of the variable in your alert if you configure your widget this way, because both actions will be executed together. However, if you do want to access the value of the variable in your alert, then you have to *chain* these two actions together. This will ensure that the Show Alert action is executed *after* the Store Value action has finished executing.

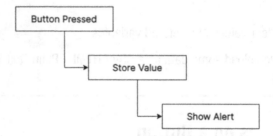

Figure 2-22. *Chained actions on a button*

Chaining is achieved by attaching actions to the On success or On failure callbacks of an action (Figure 2-23).

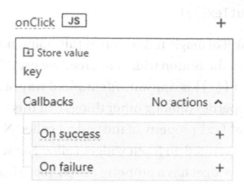

Figure 2-23. *Callbacks on a button*

Similar to adding actions on the onClick handler of a button, you can add multiple actions to the On success and On failure callbacks of each action. The actions added to these callbacks can have subsequent actions added to *their* On success and On failure callbacks too!

Note   While there is no theoretical limit to the levels of chaining you can do with Appsmith actions, it is generally advisable to limit chains to two or three actions at a maximum. Any more and you risk your UI becoming frozen for a long time, undermining the user experience of your application.

For the Greetings Application

For the Greetings application, create a new Button widget, and rename it **Submit**. Set its tooltip to display the text "Submit Form." Next, add an action to the button's onClick handler so that it displays an alert of type Success. In the Message field of the Alert configuration, enter the following text:

```
Hola, {{Name.inputText}}!
```

Sure, it may look like magic text to you at this point, but this piece of code is simply asking the Button widget to greet the user! The double-curly-brace notation {{ }} is Appsmith's standard way of referring to different widget properties (among other things). In this case, we are referring to the `inputText` property of the widget called Name.

As you recall, we created an Input widget called Name in the previous section. Every Input widget has a property called `inputText`, which contains whatever value the user enters into the widget when they are using your application.[11] If the user entered their name in the input widget and then clicked on the "Submit" button, your toy application will create an alert, greeting them.

Move the widget just below the **Name** widget and remove any unnecessary widgets from the Canvas Editor.

Running the Greetings Application

At this point in time, we have configured the Greetings application, and we're ready to run it! To do so, click on the "Preview" button on the top right of the Canvas Editor (Figure 2-24).

ⓘ PREVIEW   ⚓ SHARE   🅐 DEPLOY ⌄

Figure 2-24. *Preview your application*

If all goes well, you should see your application on screen in all its (simple) glory! See Figure 2-25.

---

[11] We will learn more about various such properties of different widgets in Chapter 4.

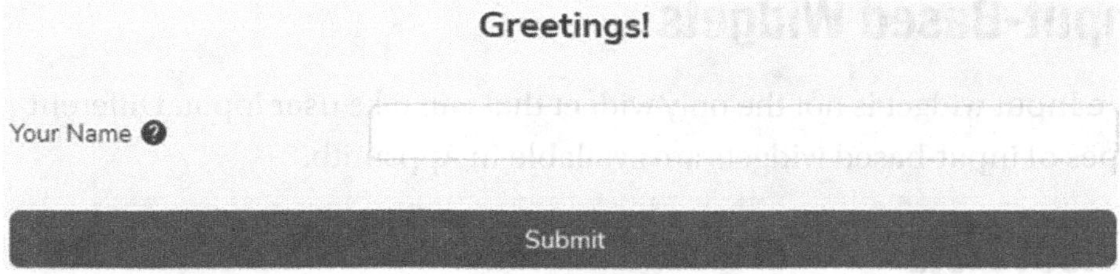

Greetings!

Your Name ❓

Submit

Figure 2-25. *The Greetings application*

Go ahead—enter your name, click on the "Submit" button, and enjoy the fruits of your labor!

Other Appsmith Widgets

By now, you should be feeling confident enough to begin exploring the rest of the Appsmith widgets on your own. The intuitive design of the platform and the hands-on experience you've gained so far should empower you to experiment with the various widgets available. Remember, the Canvas Editor is your sandbox. Feel free to drag and drop widgets, play around with their properties, and create interfaces that best suit your needs.

Each widget has its unique features and functionalities that can be leveraged to build powerful applications. The more you experiment with the different widgets, the better you'll understand their capabilities and how you can harness their potential.

In the following section, we will provide brief descriptions of some of the most widely used Appsmith widgets. This will give you a high-level understanding of what each widget does, along with some of its key functionalities. However, don't limit yourself to just these widgets. Appsmith's widget library is expansive, and each widget serves a specific purpose, providing you with a wide range of tools to build your perfect application.

Input-Based Widgets

The Input widget is not the only widget that can take user input. Different types of input-based widgets are available in Appsmith.

Select Lists

Appsmith provides four widgets that let the users select options from a list:

- **Select**: This is the simplest of the select lists. It allows the user to select one option out of a list of items, complete with a search box to filter items.

- **Tree Select**: This widget also allows the user to select one item, but allows those items to be laid out in a tree-style manner, where an item can have sub-items, and those sub-items can have their own sub-items.

- **Multi Select**: This widget presents a linear list to the user, with an ability to select more than one item from it.

- **Multi Tree Select**: Multiple items can be selected from a list, which are laid out in a tree-style manner.

The items displayed inside a select list can either be static or be bound to dynamic values.

Non-Text Inputs

Sometimes, user input need not be textual. You might want to have your users provide inputs by checking some boxes, picking dates, providing star ratings, or even recording their voice! For such scenarios, Appsmith provides a number of widgets that can take inputs via different means:

- **Checkbox** and **Checkbox Group**: These widgets render checkboxes for the user to check off. A user can check multiple boxes inside a checkbox group.

- **Radio Group**: This widget provides a group of radio buttons, only one of which can be selected at one time.

- **Switch** and **Switch Group**: A switch can be either on or off, and consequently, these widgets can be used to take Boolean inputs from the user.

- **File Picker**: A file-picker widget allows your users to upload files into your application. You can even parse those files inside Appsmith, as we will see in Chapter 4.

- **Audio Recorder**, **Camera**, and **Code Scanner**: These widgets can enable your users to record audio, click a picture, and scan a barcode or a QR code. Note that, due to the sensitive nature of microphone and camera hardware, your end users will have to provide explicit permission to Appsmith for accessing these devices before using these widgets to provide input.

Interaction-Based Widgets

Appsmith also offers a few different avatars of the Button widget to induce interactivity in your application:

- **Icon Button**: The Icon Button widget behaves *exactly* like the Button widget, except that in place of a label, you can select an icon to be displayed. This makes the Icon Button widget smaller than the Button widget, while offering the same functionality as its larger counterpart.

- **Menu Button**: The Menu Button widget opens a menu when clicked, each item of which behaves like a Button. You can assign actions to each menu item in the same way as you would to a Button or an Icon Button widget.

- **Button Group**: This widget renders a row of buttons together, each of which can behave as either a button (i.e., actions can directly be assigned to it) or a menu button (i.e., it opens a menu, whose items can have actions assigned to them).

Forms

Ever since the advent of web, a web-based form has been the default way of getting input from users on a website or a web application. A low-code application is no different, so Appsmith provides two widgets to create forms. See the following:

- **Form**: The Form widget is nothing but a composite widget consisting of a Text widget to display the form's title, and a set of Submit and Reset Buttons, all contained within a standard Container widget. You can add elements of your form inside the form, and use appropriate actions on the buttons to submit the data. This widget does not provide any built-in form-like functionality.

- **JSON Form**: The JSON Form widget also comes with a container and submit and reset buttons, but makes it much easier to include input widgets inside your form. Unlike the Form widget, you can use the convenient "Add a New Field" button on the widget's right-hand sidebar to add any kind of input widget as part of your form. You still have to bind the "Submit" and the "Reset" buttons correctly, though.

Output-Based Widgets

In addition to providing various ways to input data from the user, Appsmith also provides various ways to display data in your application. Earlier in the chapter we looked at the Text widget, which can be used to display textual data on screen. A number of other interesting options are also available to you for all your data display needs inside Appsmith.

Note   It is possible to use all the following output-based widgets to display static data or to bind them to a data source to display dynamic data.

- **Table**: A table is best suited to display rows and columns of data in your Appsmith application. The Table widget comes fully equipped with features like full-text search of table data, filters, pagination, and the ability to download the displayed data as either a CSV or an Excel file.

- **Image**: Use this widget when you want to speak a thousand words! The Image widget can display any image hosted on the internet or your company intranet. If a URL is not available, you can even provide the Base64 representation of your image.

- **Audio** and **Video**: These widgets let you specify an Audio or a Video URL, which can then be played inside your application.

- **Stats Box**: The Stats Box is a composite widget consisting of a few Text widgets and an Icon Button widget arranged inside a Container. You can bind each of these widgets to different data sources and present information in an elegant manner.

- **Progress**: The Progress widget allows you to show real-time progress of a long-running task in your application.

Summary

And there we have it! In this chapter, we embarked on a journey into the world of Appsmith's Canvas Editor and widgets. We started by understanding the Canvas Editor, an intuitive and versatile tool that allows us to design and modify our applications visually. The Canvas Editor's drag-and-drop mechanism enabled us to experiment freely, offering a practical, hands-on way to learn about Appsmith's capabilities.

We then delved into three fundamental widgets: the Text, the Input, and the Button. We explored their properties, functionalities, and how they interact with other components of an application. Using these widgets, we successfully created the Greetings application, providing us with a real-world example of how these widgets work together to create functional, interactive applications.

Lastly, we took a brief tour of the other widgets offered by Appsmith, laying the foundation for you to explore these widgets more in-depth on your own. The power of Appsmith truly lies in its wide array of widgets, each designed to accomplish specific tasks and provide various functionalities.

The journey doesn't stop here, though. Remember, the most effective way to learn is by doing. So, we encourage you to take what you've learned in this chapter and apply it by trying out different widgets and creating your own applications.

We hope you've found this chapter informative and inspiring. Now, go forth and create. The canvas is yours to shape!

CHAPTER 3

Working with Datasources

Enterprises are creating massive amounts of data on all operating platforms, like cloud infrastructure, on-premises databases, and at-edge devices. All this data can be classified as structured, semi-structured, or unstructured and stored in several types of store, like Relational Database Management System (RDBMS), datalake, NoSQL, time-series DB, and so on. Businesses can solve several challenges and unlock potential value by making this data transparently available beyond the primary stakeholders. However, low-cost development platforms (LCDPs), facilitating citizen development, must be able to read and update the full assortment of company data.

In the previous chapter, you created user interfaces for Appsmith applications. In this chapter, you will work with the various datastore integrations available in Appsmith. By the end of the chapter, you can be confident in reading data, transforming it, displaying insights, and updating it. These features will provide foundations for unlocking values of organizational data.

Datasource Principles

It can be harrowing to work with a tool if you are unaware of its guidelines. Without this knowledge, it is very chaotic and frustrating to deliver a working solution. It impacts the entire cycle of development, like requirement capturing, team onboarding, fixing bugs, and debugging issues. However, knowing these guidelines can lead to efficient solutions with minimal bugs and errors. Moreover, it helps in building consistent workarounds for custom extensions, unsupported out-of-the-box. In this section, let's first understand the principles of integrating the Appsmith datasource.

Data Binding

In Chapter 2, you used the Canvas Editor to build an application user interface (UI) by pulling in different widgets. The UI components must be integrated with datasources to capture and render data. Appsmith provides a concise and powerful declarative binding system to link data to its UI component. The binding relies on three parts: the widget name specified by the developer, data properties supported by the widget, and the fields of your data. Following are a few examples:

- An input box for email named `userEmail`. Then you can determine/specify its value by referring to `userEmail.text`.

- If there is a dropdown for countries named as `countryName`, then you can determine the selected value by referring to `countryName.selectedOptionValue`.

- If there is a table for employee records named `employeeData`, then you can determine the selected `employeeId` value by referring to `employeeData.selectedRow.empId`.

You must refer to the appropriate widget properties for reading data and displaying data. Please refer to Appsmith documentation for the exact property names.

Naming UI widgets correctly is essential for functional data binding. Moreover, a team should agree on a naming methodology that can enforce uniform names and readable code.

A lowercase naming scheme is recommended for UI widgets. If you have multiple words in a name, separate the words with hyphens instead of switching to camelCase.

Native Query

Every datastore supports a query language for storing and processing information. The native query language is often optimized for execution and offers several capabilities, like JOINS in RDBMS, JSON lookup in NoSQL, etc. Appsmith does not provide a unified query language over the supported heterogeneous datasources. Instead, Appsmith supports the execution of native queries against your configured datasource, thereby allowing you to take full advantage of all database capabilities. You will work with the Query Editor in later sections of this chapter.

Queries are responsible for loading data as a JSON object array. In NoSql DBs like MongoDB and Elastic, the data is just a list of objects, while in RDBMS, each object is presented as a row and each key as a column. This data is presented in UI widgets. As discussed, the data must be bound to individual properties of the UI widget. Appsmith allows you to transform the query data to match the UI widget's expected data.

Data Callbacks

Appsmith executes all data operations Create Read Update Delete (CRUD) as queries. These queries are long-running network operations. They are executed asynchronously without blocking the main UI thread, so the UI

remains responsive to user actions. All queries have a delayed execution
that will eventually complete in either of the following ways, as shown in
Figure 3-1:

- A successful completion, with some data

- A failure, with some error code/details

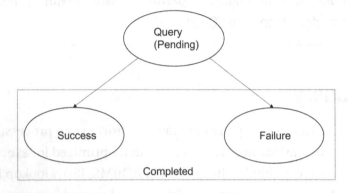

***Figure 3-1.** Query states*

These states are denoted with onSuccess and onFailure methods of
query execution. After successfully completing (insert and update query),
you may fetch the data again by re-executing the data load query.

Pagination

Large databases can quickly generate thousands of records for specific
queries. It can lead to several issues, like performance concerns and
poor user experience. Fetching non-paginated items increases memory
footprint and can lead to server and client-side application crashes.

Appsmith can optimally process up to 5MB of query response.
This means in a table with 20 columns, where each column is a
varchar(50), you can select around 5,000 rows.

Pagination of data is often required to split the large dataset into pages. These pages contain limited data and can gradually fetch and display records to the user. If you are working with RDBMS like MySQL and Postgres, then the following SQL features are used to provide pagination:

- The LIMIT clause specifies the number of rows to fetch from the database.

- The OFFSET clause specifies the number of rows of the result table to skip before any rows are retrieved and must be used with the LIMIT clause.

The OFFSET clause instructs the server where to start returning rows within the query result.

```
SELECT * FROM transactions LIMIT 100 OFFSET 10
```

The preceding query returns 100 rows, and specifying OFFSET 10 instructs the server to skip the first ten rows of the query results. The concept of pagination is implemented with different keywords in different datasources; e.g., in MongoDB, you will use the SKIP and LIMIT query parameters for pagination. As part of the datasource integration, you will work with these pagination parameters later in this chapter.

Search and Filter

Searching is the process of retrieving records matching user-provided criteria. Filtering is the process of limiting records on one of their shown attribute values. These are two different UI operations; e.g., in MS Excel, you can filter based on one of the column values, while a search can be used to look up across different columns. These operations are supported by individual datasource queries, as follows:

- In SQL, you can use the LIKE operation for search and the equal operation (=) to filter records.

- In MongoDB, you can use the filter query option for both search and filter.

As part of the datasource integration, you will work with these query parameters later in this chapter.

Datasource Connectors

Enterprises have heterogeneous datasources as part of the entire organization's IT landscape. Appsmith provides out-of-the-box integrations with several widely used databases. This pluggable capability, without any necessary setup, allows you to read application data, transform it, and show results.

To work with datasources, first access the Appsmith dashboard (Figure 3-2). As discussed in Chapter 2, the dashboard lists all applications created by you. Select a sample application to access the application development console.

Figure 3-2. *Appsmith dashboard*

Appsmith's application-side navigation bar shows the list of available datasources. The menu also provides the option to add a new datasource.

Hands-on: Movie Rental Scenario

HELLO PICTURES is a movie rental business. They have stores across different locations and provide movies for rent. The technology landscape has applications that can perform several functions, like onboarding customers; looking up movies based on actors, genres, or titles; and creating bookings. You are tasked to build bookings and earnings dashboards using Appsmith.

HELLO PICTURES is using MySQL as its back end. The Sakila sample database shared by the MySQL team accurately captures the required schema. As a prerequisite, please ensure you have access to a MySQL instance, say at host mysql.hellopictures and port 3306.

Download the Sakila database from https://dev.mysql.com/doc/index-other.html. The zipped artifact contains DDL and DML scripts. Execute the sakila-schema.sql script to create the database structure, and execute the sakila-data.sql script to populate the database tables by using the following commands:

```
mysql> SOURCE sakila-schema.sql;
mysql> SOURCE sakila-data.sql;
```

Replace the paths to the sakila-schema.sql and sakila-data.sql files with the actual paths on your system.

MySQL Connector

Appsmith connectors determine the source of every piece of data. This data can be pulled from several sources, like APIs, databases, data warehouses, etc. Thus there are over 20 connectors in Appsmith that provide various integrations. As discussed earlier, start by clicking the Datasource plus(+) icon in the left-hand navigation bar. The action opens the catalog of available integrations (Figure 3-3).

Figure 3-3. *Datasource catalog*

Click on the MySQL icon to add the corresponding configuration. The MySQL configuration page asks for the details listed in Table 3-1.

Table 3-1. *MySQL Cconfiguration Attributes*

Datasource Name	Provide a meaningful name for the added configuration.
Connection Mode	Configures the read or write privileges for the connector
Hostname	Specify the location of the database as a hostname or IP address.
Port	Specify the port for the database.
Schema Name	Specify a specific schema to use, or user-associated schema will be used.
Username	Configures the user credentials for the connector
Password	Configures the user credentials for the connector
SSL Configuration	Specifies if SSL is enforced by the database for the connection

You can also validate the details by clicking the "Test" button. Any connection error will raise a popup with the required error details. Once validated, click the "Save" button to add the datasource named HelloPictures (Figure 3-4). The new datasource appears on the side navigation bar and lists the tables existing in the corresponding database.

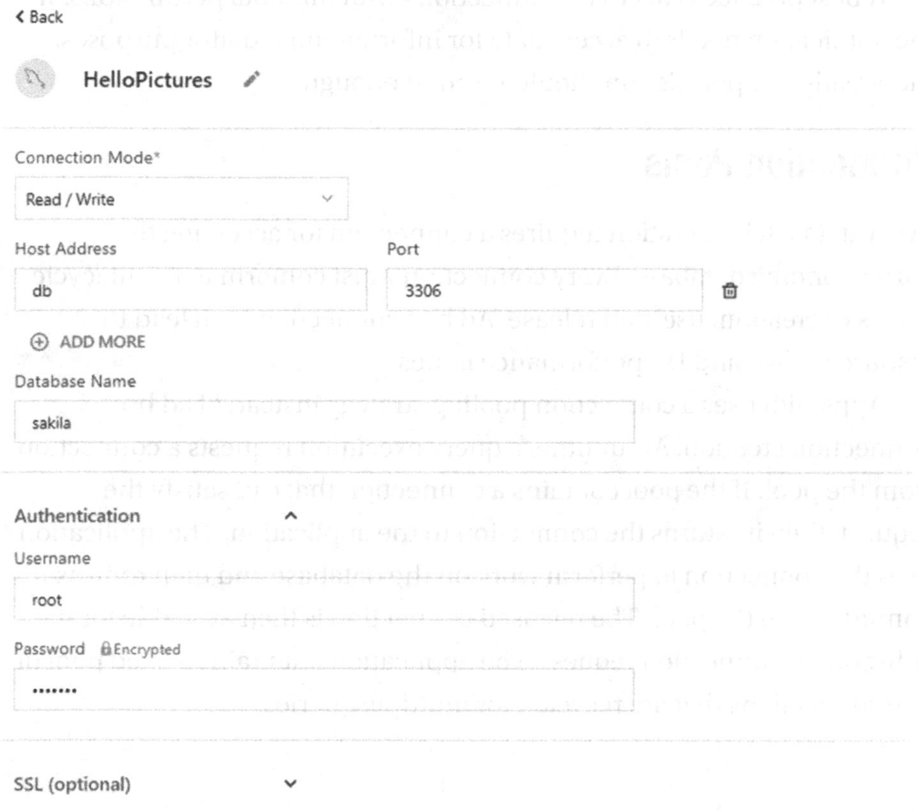

Figure 3-4. *MySQL Connector config*

Connection Mode

A datasource setup in Appsmith is accomplished by providing datasource credentials, schema configuration, and a connection mode. The mode is permission granted to update and insert data. It will govern how queries are executed against the provided datasource. Appsmith supports the following modes:

- Readonly

- Read-write

A best practice is to create connections with minimal permissions. If the application needs to access data for information radiator purposes, then read-only permission should be good enough.

Connection Pools

Every data fetch operation requires a connection for accessing the corresponding database. Every connection must conform to the lifecycle stages of creation, use, and release. Ad hoc connections can lead to resource usage and DB performance issues.

Appsmith uses a connection pooling strategy instead of ad hoc connection creation. At runtime, a query execution requests a connection from the pool. If the pool contains a connection that can satisfy the request, then it returns the connection to the application. The application uses the connection to perform work on the database and then returns the connection to the pool. The released connection is then available for the subsequent connection request. The application maintains a fixed pool of five connections that are recycled for multiple queries.

Data Queries

After adding a datasource, you can build queries to create, select, update, or delete data. The query section is part of the side navigation. Click on the plus(+) icon to add a new query. It opens a sub-menu (Figure 3-5) that lists the available datasources.

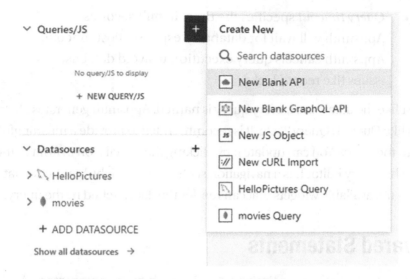

Figure 3-5. *Add querries*

Click on the named MySQL datasource that was added in the preceding section. This action opens the Query Editor. It also provides several query templates for different operations. You can either click one of the templates and modify the query snippet or start with an empty editor. The Query Editor also has a Settings tab that provides the following options to control query execution:

- By default, all queries are executed when the widget is rendered. Alternatively, you can configure the query to always execute on page load. This is not recommended but can be preferred for executing slow queries.

- *Prepared statement* configures the query as a SQL template which is executed efficiently by passing values as parameters.

- *Query timeout* specifies the time, in milliseconds,
  Appsmith will wait for database response. Post timeout,
  Appsmith cancels query execution to avoid database
  issues like record locks.

Just like the datasource, every query is named. Appsmith generates abstract names like Query 1, Query 2, etc. It is recommended to provide a meaningful name to the query. You can update it by clicking the pencil icon in front of the name. The Query Editor has a navigation section on the right-hand side that suggests the available widgets that can render the data fetched by the query.

Prepared Statements

Prepared statements are optimized queries with query parameters. A prepared SQL query can perform all SQL operations while offering the following benefits:

- The query only needs to be parsed once by the
  database. However, it can be executed multiple
  times with the same or different parameters. When a
  query is executed, the database analyzes, compiles,
  and optimizes its execution plan before running it.
  A complex query can take time in this process and
  noticeably slow the application on repeated executions
  with different parameters. A prepared statement avoids
  repeating the analyze/compile/optimize cycle, thus
  resulting in faster execution.

- The parameters to prepared statements don't need
  to be escaped and validated. The database driver
  automatically performs this. This helps to prevent
  SQL injection attacks, a technique used to exploit
  applications that utilize user-specified data in SQL
  statements, like the where clause.

While a prepared query offers benefits, it must bind the parameters to appropriate data types. Improper type binding often leads to SQL failures and data issues. Appsmith has auto-detection to determine database types based on the data type configured in the widget. Turn off the prepared statements feature in case of problems in binding the correct data type. Appsmith will inject parameters using JS (interpolation).

Hands-on: Movie Rental Dashboard

As a member of the ops team at HELLO PICTURES, you are tasked to build a Movie performance dashboard with the following capabilities:

1. Determine the top 10 movies regarding the number of bookings and the revenue earned, respectively.

2. List all movies available in the system.

SQL details are well beyond the scope of this book. This chapter will only cover the final SQL with some brief notes on the key SQL operators. Please refer to MySQL documentation for details.

A dashboard is usually a single-page application designed to help users understand what areas require attention. Thus, it should project data with adequate charts and search capabilities.

Bookings Data

Start by creating a query named `film_bookings` under the `HelloPictures` database connector. As per the application schema, you need a SQL `JOIN` operation on bookings, inventory, and film tables.

```
SELECT  film.title  , count(*) as bookings from rental
  INNER JOIN inventory ON rental.inventory_id = inventory.
  inventory_id
  INNER JOIN film ON inventory.film_id = film.film_id
  group by film.film_id  order by bookings desc limit 10;
```

The preceding query performs the joins and then aggregates the data on the film_id column to determine the top rented movies. It uses the LIMIT operator to pick the top ten items. You can execute the query from the editor (Figure 3-6) by clicking the "Run" button in the top right corner. All results are shown either in the Response console or the Error console, displayed below the Query Editor.

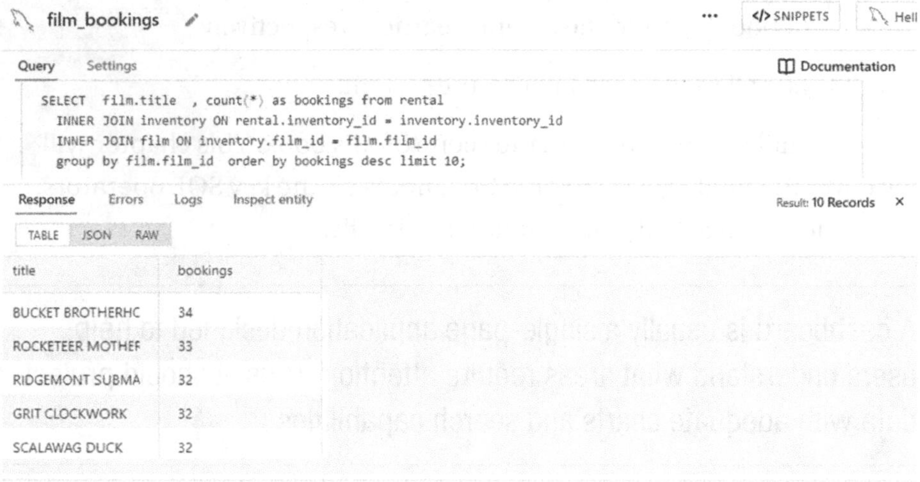

Figure 3-6. *Bookings query*

Chart Widget

Charts can be used to display the movie booking data in a visual manner. It is often easier to comprehend information in a chart rather than reading blocks of text. The Query Editor has a right-hand navigation that provides a list of compatible widgets for the query data. You can name it as

filmbookings by clicking the pencil icon above the right navigation. Select
the Chart widget from the navigation menu. It will add a Chart widget
to the Canvas Editor with the required configuration. The following are
important properties of the Chart widget:

- chart-type: By default a column chart is added.
  Appsmith provides several other chart types, like pie
  chart, line chart, etc. Select the bar chart as it can show
  the data in a comparative manner.

- chart series: The series property configures the data
  mapping between the x- and y-axes on the chart. The
  generated mapping is good enough. Additionally, you
  can provide the series name, which defaults to Sales,
  and color.

Additionally there are Axis and General properties, which configure
chart labels and the title. Update the chart title as Booking Report and
Axis as Movies (Figure 3-7).

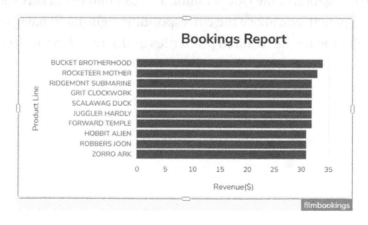

Figure 3-7. *Bookings bar chart*

Revenue Data

Create a new query under the HelloPictures database connector and name it film_revenue. This is very similar to the Bookings query. It is a SQL JOIN operation on bookings, inventory, and film tables.

```
SELECT  film.title  , count(*) * film.rental_rate as revenue
from rental
INNER JOIN inventory ON rental.inventory_id = inventory.
inventory_id
INNER JOIN film ON inventory.film_id = film.film_id
group by film.film_id order by revenue desc limit 10;
```

Unlike the Bookings query, the Revenue query considers rental_rate to compute total earnings. You can execute the query from the editor by clicking the "Run" button in the top right corner. All results are shown either in the Response console or the Error console, displayed below the Query Editor.

Next, add a chart by clicking on the Chart Type widget from the right-hand side navigation of the Query Editor. You can name it filmrevenue by clicking the pencil icon above the corresponding right-hand navigation (Figure 3-8). Update the required properties as discussed in the previous section.

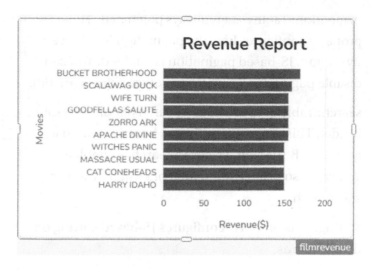

Figure 3-8. *Revenue bar chart*

Films Data

Create a new query under the `HelloPictures` database connector and name it `films`. The query lists all records from the Film table.

```
SELECT * FROM film order by film_id desc
```

Next, add a table by clicking on the Table widget from the right-hand navigation of the Query Editor. You can name it `filmlist` by clicking the pencil icon above the right-hand navigation. Only limited rows are shown in the table (Figure 3-9). You can resize the table for more data rows by dragging the bounds. The following are important properties of the Table widget:

- data columns: This property lists all columns available in data. You can toggle the visibility of a column. Additionally, there is an Editable checkbox, which enables record-level data updates.

- pagination: Table data is always paginated. This property configures how the pagination is achieved. By default, JS-based pagination is enabled. You can disable pagination or switch to server-side pagination.

- search: Table data provides a search bar on the table header. This property configures how the search is achieved. By default, JS-based search is enabled. You can also disable the search or switch to server-side search.

- sorting: This property configures JS-based sorting on data columns

film_id	title	description	release_year	language_id	original_langu...	rental_duration
1000	ZORRO ARK	A Intrepid Panora...	2006	1		3
999	ZOOLANDER FICT...	A Fateful Reflectio...	2006	1		5
998	ZHIVAGO CORE	A Fateful Yarn of a...	2006	1		6
997	YOUTH KICK	A Touching Drama...	2006	1		4
996	YOUNG LANGUA...	A Unbelieveable Y...	2006	1		6
995	YENTL IDAHO	A Amazing Displa...	2006	1		5
994	WYOMING STORM	A Awe-Inspiring P...	2006	1		6
993	WRONG BEHAVI...	A Emotional Saga ...	2006	1		6
992	WRATH MILE	A Intrepid Reflecti...	2006	1		5
991	WORST BANGER	A Thrilling Drama ...	2006	1		4

Figure 3-9. *List films*

Server-Side Pagination

The film query in the preceding section performed JS-based pagination. But that has limits, as mentioned in the pagination section. Start by updating the SQL query named Films and add the LIMIT and OFFSET operators.

```
SELECT * FROM film order by film_id desc LIMIT {{ filmlist.
pageSize }} OFFSET {{ filmlist.pageOffset }}
```

This query binds `filmlist` Table widget properties in the SQL query. Next, enable the `ServerSide Pagination` property of the `filmlist` Table widget. The feature will ask for the following additional properties:

- Total Number of Records: This is set to 0 (zero) as the application cannot determine the record count in the database. If the value is 0, the total pages are not shown in the table header. Alternatively, you can create a new count query and bind the same for the property.

- onPageChange: This property specifies the query to execute. It should not need any change.

Add another query called `film_count` to get the total number of films in the database:

```
select count(*) as total_films from film
```

Next, update the `Total Records` property of the `filmslist` Table widget to use the count (Figure 3-10). You can refer to the value using the following JSON notation:

```
{{film_count.data[0].total_films}}
```

Figure 3-10. *Configure server-side pagination*

Server-Side Search

The film query in the preceding section performed a JS-based search. But the search becomes inefficient with server-side pagination, as limited data is fetched in the query. Thus, you need to enable server-side search, which limits the search to predefined columns. Meanwhile, the JS search works on all columns. Start by updating the SQL query named `films` with the `LIKE` operator.

```
SELECT * FROM film WHERE title LIKE {{"%" + filmlist.searchText
+ "%"}} ORDER BY film_id LIMIT {{ filmlist.pageSize }} OFFSET
{{ filmlist.pageOffset }}
```

This query binds the `filmlist` Table widget properties in the SQL query. Next, disable the client-side search property of `filmlist` Table widget. Update the `onSearchTextChanged` property of the `filmslist` Table widget to execute the `films` query. The search should function as expected

(Figure 3-11). Additionally, you should also update the pagination query with the where clause and execute it from the onSearchTextChanged property of the filmslist widget.

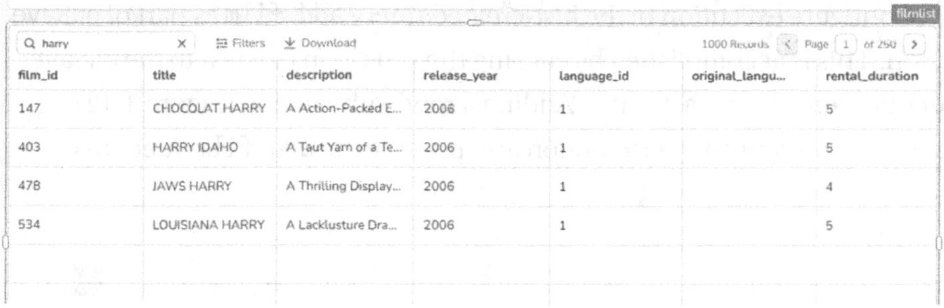

Figure 3-11. *Configure server-side search*

Add Film

A Table widget is used to list film data in the preceding section. The same widget also supports data updates and data inserts. This makes the Table widget quite versatile. As a first step, you must select which columns are editable; i.e., which allows the application user to change/update the data. The columns menu, part of the right-hand navigation, provides a checkbox to achieve this. Select the filmslist Table widget and mark film_id, title, description, and language_id as editable.

Next, move to the "Adding a row" sub-section in the right-hand navigation sidebar and enable the feature. A new "Add row" button, with a plus icon, will be shown over the data table. Next, you must configure the onSave action to execute an INSERT query.

Create a new INSERT query, add_film, under the HelloPictures database connector. The query should have a simple INSERT script, but it needs to pick the values from the new row added to the filmlist widget.

```
INSERT INTO film (film_id, title, description, language_id)
VALUES ( {{ filmlist.newRow.film_id}},
```

```
{{ filmlist.newRow.title }},
{{ filmlist.newRow.description }},
{{ filmlist.newRow.language_id }} );
```

Configure execution of the just-created query add_film as part of onSave action. This is accomplished by clicking the plus icon (+) next to the onSave sidebar menu item, part of the "Adding a row" sub-section (Figure 3-12). Select the "Execute a query" option and provide the add_film query name.

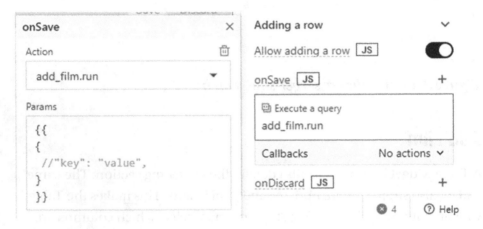

Figure 3-12. *Insert film*

Data Callbacks

You should be able to add new films, but the newly added data is displayed once the page reloads. A page reload executes all the required queries to fetch the data. The same thing needs to be accomplished after successful persistence. Appsmith supports success and failure callbacks for every query execution.

In the preceding section, the add_film query execution was configured as part of the "Adding a row" sub-section. The sub-section also provides a callback configuration for the selected query. Click on the callback link underneath the query name to get options for OnSuccess and Onfailure callback events (Figure 3-13). Specify the `films` query execution as part of the `OnSuccess` event.

Figure 3-13. *Refresh films*

The preceding configuration will execute the `films` query and reload the table after successful execution.

Update Data

The `filmlist` table has editable rows with an additional column at the end specifying `Save` / `Discard` actions. The column is available as part of the columns section in the right-hand navigation sidebar. You must configure the "Save" button to execute an update script. Click the cog icon to open the settings corresponding to the Save/Discard buttons. Next, you must provide the data `UPDATE` query as part of the save action. This is similar to configuring `INSERT SQL`, as discussed in the preceding section. Alternatively, you can also turn off the visibility of the Save/Discard column by clicking the eye icon. It effectively disables the update data feature.

91

MongoDB Connector

MongoDB is a popular NoSQL choice for organizations aiming to develop high-throughput, data-driven applications. It enables you to model data in JSON-like document format (BSON). The format can represent rich, hierarchical data structures without the need for joins as imposed by relational databases. The data is also looked up using JSON-based queries. The following section discusses guidelines for integrating Appsmith with MongoDB and fetching data for various purposes. The discussion is limited to the required details only. Complete information about MongoDB and queries is well beyond this book's scope.

Import Collections

HELLO PICTURES is using MongoDB for its application backend. The database has three collections for their store, customer, and film data. Each of these documents consists of nested structures to represent data correctly. As a prerequisite, please make sure you have access to a MongoDB instance, say at host mongodb.hellopictures and port 27017.

Then, download the Sakila MongoDB database from https://github. com/rahul0208/sakila/archive/refs/tags/0.1.zip. The zipped artifact contains three JSON files, one for each collection. Use the following commands to restore the collections for JSON data:

```
$ mongoimport --uri mongodb://mongodb.hellopictures:27017
/?directConnection=true --username mongo --password mongo
--authenticationDatabase=test --collection films films.json
$ mongoimport --uri mongodb://mongodb.hellopictures:27017
/?directConnection=true --username mongo --password mongo
--authenticationDatabase=test --collection stores stores.json
$ mongoimport --uri mongodb://mongodb.hellopictures:27017
/?directConnection=true --username mongo --password mongo
--authenticationDatabase=test --collection customers  customers.json
```

Replace the paths to the `stores.json`, `customers.json`, and `films.json` files with the actual paths on your system.

Configure Connector

Appsmith provides a datasource connector for integrating MongoDB. Move to the new datasource page by clicking the plus (+) icon for datasource. Click on the MongoDB icon and provide the details listed in Table 3-2.

Table 3-2. *MongoDB Configuration Properties*

Datasource Name	Provide a meaningful name for the added configuration.
Connection Mode	Configures the read or write privileges for the connector
Connection Type	Specifies the kind of Mongo connection
Hostname	Specify the location of the database as a hostname or IP address.
Port	Specify the port for the database.
Default Database Name	Specify a database to use, or a user-associated schema will be used.
Authentication Database	Configures the user-associated database
Authentication Username	Configures the user credentials for the connector
Authentication Password	Configures the user credentials for the connector
Authentication Type	Specifies the type of authentication
SSL Configuration	Specifies if SSL is enforced by the database for the connection

Create a connection named mongoMovies with the required details. The new datasource appears on the side navigation bar and lists the available collections in the respective database.

Data Queries

Create a query named mongo_film_bookings under the mongoMovies datasource connector. The customer document has a nested structure where rental information is captured. The rental information includes film and payment details. Thus, an aggregate query on the rental film details fetches the required data.

```
[{"$project": {"Rentals": 1}},
 {$unwind: "$Rentals"},
 {$group: { _id: "$Rentals.Film Title",    count: { $sum : 1 }}},
 { $sort : { count : -1 } }]
```

The preceding JSON query creates an aggregate pipeline with the following steps:

- Project: Extracts the Rentals array from the customer document

- Unwind: Flattens the Rentals array into individual data items

- Group: Buckets data based on the film title from each rental data item. Additionally, counts the number of items.

- Sort: Orders the data in descending count

The query also uses the LIMIT method to pick the top ten items. Save the query and add a bar chart as discussed in the "Bookings Data" section.

Next, add a query named mongo_film_revenue under the mongoMovies datasource connector. This will be similar to the bookings query where aggregation is required on the rental information. The data bucketing on the film title must generate the review by using a sum operation instead of the count operation of bookings queries.

```
[{"$project": {"Rentals": 1}},
 { $unwind: "$Rentals"},
 {$group: {_id: "$Rentals.Film Title", amount: { $sum : {$round
 : [ {$reduce: { input: "$Rentals.Payments",initialValue: 0, in:
{$add: ["$$value", "$$this.Amount"]} }}, 0]}}}},
 { $sort : { amount : -1 } }]
```

The preceding JSON query creates an aggregate pipeline (Figure 3-14) with the following steps :

- Project: Extracts the Rentals array from the Customer document.

- Unwind: Flattens the Rentals array into individual data items

- Group: Buckets data based on the film title from each rental data item. Additionally, computes a sum operation by aggregating the payment amount

- Sort: Orders the data in descending count.

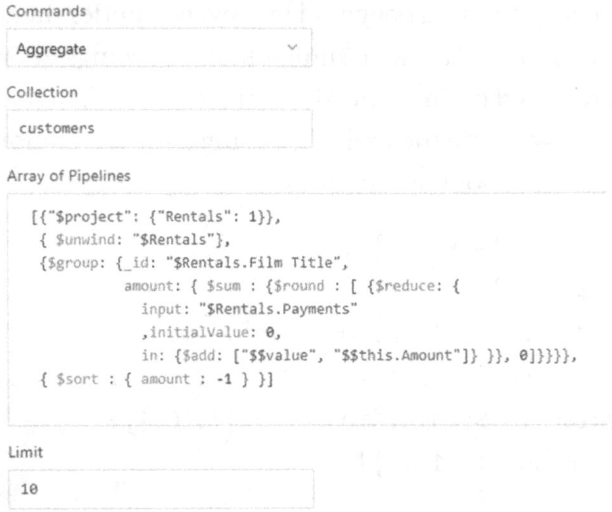

Commands

Aggregate

Collection

customers

Array of Pipelines

```
[{"$project": {"Rentals": 1}},
 { $unwind: "$Rentals"},
 {$group: {_id: "$Rentals.Film Title",
         amount: { $sum : {$round : [ {$reduce: {
             input: "$Rentals.Payments"
             ,initialValue: 0,
             in: {$add: ["$$value", "$$this.Amount"]} }}, 0]}}}},
 { $sort : { amount : -1 } }]
```

Limit

10

Figure 3-14. *Aggregate payments*

The query uses the LIMIT method to pick the top ten items. Save the query and add a bar chart, as discussed in the "Bookings Data" section.

Next, build a find documents query on the films collection and name it mongo_films. There are no data filters; thus, the query is an empty JSON({}). Configure the sort method to perform descending order based on _id attribute ({"_id": -1}). Save the query and add a Table widget from the right-hand navigation, as discussed in the "Films Data" section.

Enable server-side pagination on the newly added Table widget. As discussed earlier, you need to perform the following changes:

- Configure the Limit method of the mongo_films query with {{films_mongo.pageSize}} value.

- Configure the Skip method of the mongo_films query with {{films_mongo.pageOffset}} value.

- Configure the Total Count property of films_mongo Table widget to execute a count query to determine the number of documents in the Films collection.

Lastly, you can configure server-side search by passing appropriate criteria in the query method.

Summary

Applications in Appsmith can load data using datasources. This chapter lists Appsmith's native integration with key databases. The integration is quite minimalistic but based on a few conventions. These conventions were discussed in the beginning to provide the necessary foundation. Later in the chapter, there was hands-on integration with MySQL and Mongo databases for the movie-rental scenario. The problem statement led to the generation of a dashboard with SELECT/ INSERT/ UPDATE / AGGREGATION capabilities. The next chapter will provide hands-on experience with multi-page and workflow-based applications.

CHAPTER 4

Creating Application Flows

In our journey through Appsmith so far, we have covered the basics, familiarized ourselves with the Canvas Editor, and learned how to work with databases. Now, it's time to elevate our game. Let's roll up our sleeves and dive into creating more complex application flows using a multi-page application model.

So, let's begin this exciting journey, creating and configuring page layouts, building complex UIs, establishing data connections, and formulating intricate workflows. Let's create an application that is not just functional, but also provides a seamless user experience and meets the needs of a demanding business environment.

Adding Interactivity

In Appsmith, you can write JavaScript code to add custom functionality and interactivity to your applications. The code can be added within various widgets or in the form of API actions and lifecycle hooks. Appsmith provides a powerful and intuitive code editor with syntax highlighting, auto-completion, and error checking to streamline your coding experience.

© Rahul Sharma and Rajat Arora 2023
R. Sharma and R. Arora, *Low-Code Development with Appsmith*,
https://doi.org/10.1007/978-1-4842-9813-8_4

You can leverage JavaScript to manipulate data, perform calculations, make API requests, handle events, and more, allowing you to build dynamic and responsive applications tailored to your specific needs. With Appsmith's integrated JavaScript capabilities, you have the flexibility to extend the functionality of your app and create custom workflows effortlessly.

Appsmith provides three different ways to write code while building your app; namely, using the mustache syntax, as an Immediately Invoked Function Expression (IIFE), and within a JS object. We will introduce each of these methods in the following sections.

The Mustache Syntax

The simplest way to write code in Appsmith is to use the *mustache syntax*. Mustache is a templating language[1] that allows you to embed variables, expressions, and function calls directly within your HTML or widget properties. By using double curly braces {{ }}, you can easily reference and interpolate JavaScript code within your templates. This enables you to fetch data from APIs, manipulate data, apply conditional logic, and format values.

Let's do a small experiment to see the mustache syntax in action. Drag a new Button widget on the Canvas Editor, and then find its onClick handler on the right-hand sidebar (Figure 4-1). You will notice that it is a dropdown at the moment. However, if you click on the little **JS** button right next to its name, the dropdown will be replaced by a text field.

---

[1] You can read more about templating languages and processors here: https://en.wikipedia.org/wiki/Template_processor

Figure 4-1. *Associating JavaScript with a widget's behavior*

Write the following code in the text field:

```
{{ showAlert("You clicked a button!"); }}
```

Next, preview the app and click on the button you just created. A message will pop up on top of your screen (Figure 4-2).

Figure 4-2. *The Appsmith alert*

And that's it! You just wrote your first piece of Javascript code in Appsmith!

Note that you can also write multi-line Javascript expressions using the mustache syntax, something like:

```
{{
    showAlert("You clicked a button!");
    console.log("A button was clicked.");
}}
```

And this would work. Both of these statements will be executed, one after the other.

Immediately Invoked Function Expressions

An Immediately Invoked Function Expression (IIFE) is a common JavaScript design pattern that allows you to create and execute a function immediately, as soon as it's defined. The primary purpose of an IIFE is to create a private scope for the enclosed code, preventing any variable or function declarations from polluting the global namespace.

The syntax for an IIFE involves wrapping the function declaration within parentheses and immediately invoking it by adding a set of parentheses at the end. Within Appsmith, you also need to wrap the IIFE inside a pair of double curly braces:

```
{{
    (function() {
        // Code goes here
    })();
}}
```

The function within the parentheses is treated as a function expression rather than a function declaration, which means it's not accessible outside of its enclosing scope. This creates a self-contained block where variables declared inside the IIFE are limited to that scope and don't interfere with other code outside of it.

Using IIFEs, you can write complex JavaScript and have it interpolated by the Mustache processor. For example, consider the following piece of code:

```
{{
    (function() {
        if (HotdogInput.inputText == "Hotdog") {
            showAlert("It's a hotdog!");
        } else {
```

```
        showAlert("Not a hotdog!");
    }
  })();
}}
```

The preceding code can be applied to the onClick handler of a button, assuming that a Text widget called HotdogInput is available on the Canvas Editor. The code will show the alert -- It's a hotdog! if the text inside HotdogInput equals Hotdog, and Not a hotdog! in all other cases, even when the HotdogInput widget is empty.

JavaScript Objects

JavaScript objects are a fundamental part of the language that enables structured programming. They are essentially collections of key–value pairs, also known as properties, where the keys are typically strings (or symbols) and the values can be any JavaScript data type, including other objects, creating a possibility for hierarchical data structures.

A key feature of JavaScript objects is their ability to contain functions as values, which are then called *methods*. This is a building block for object-oriented programming (OOP) in JavaScript, where objects can be used to model and manage complex data structures. An object method is accessed through the object's name, followed by a period, then the method name and parentheses:

```
objectName.methodName(params);
```

JavaScript objects in Appsmith act as an interface between the visual elements of an application and its underlying data. These objects allow for a high degree of customization and control over the application's behavior, bridging the gap between the visual UI design and backend data management. They can interact with Appsmith Query and Appsmith API objects, allowing you to perform complex operations like fetching data from an API[2] when a button is clicked, or updating a database when a form is submitted. This brings a great deal of flexibility and interactivity to Appsmith applications, making them highly adaptable to a wide range of use cases.

Appsmith allows you to create JavaScript objects with a *page-level scope*. This means that you can refer to any JavaScript object associated with a page in *any* of the page's widgets and queries.

Creating JS Objects

You can create JS objects from the Entity Explorer on the left-hand sidebar (Figure 4-3). Click on the + icon next to **Queries/JS** and select **New JS Object**.

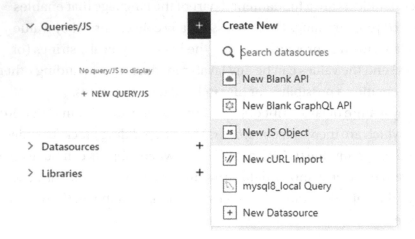

Figure 4-3. *Creating a new JS object*

---

[2] You will learn about connecting Appsmith with external APIs in Chapter 5.

Once you do that, you will be redirected to Appsmith's JavaScript Editor, with some rudimentary code displayed on screen:

```
export default {
    myVar1: [],
    myVar2: {},
    myFun1 () {
        // write code here
        // this.myVar1 = [1,2,3]
    }, async myFun2 () {
        // use async-await or promises
        // await storeValue('varName', 'hello world')
    }
}
```

This represents the basic structure of an Appsmith JS object: an export default declaration, followed by a series of key–value pairs representing variable declarations and function definitions.

Significance of Export Default

In JavaScript, the export statement is used to explicitly make functions, objects, or values available for use in other modules. This allows you to organize and share code across different files.

The export statement can be used in two main ways: named exports and default exports.

Named Exports

With named exports, you can export multiple values from a module by explicitly specifying their names. For example:

```
export const add = (a, b) => a + b;
export const subtract = (a, b) => a - b;
```

Default Exports

The default export allows you to export a single value or entity as the default export of a module. For example:

```
const multiply = (a, b) => a * b;
export default multiply;
```

In Appsmith, each JS object is treated as a JavaScript module, and it expects all variable and method declarations contained within it to be exported as its default entity export. This is why every JS object's definition is supposed to start with `export default` in Appsmith.

Appsmith JavaScript Framework

In addition to providing multiple ways to write JavaScript code inside your application, Appsmith also includes a full-featured JavaScript framework that enables you to interact with different parts of itself and the browser. You can use the various methods defined in the framework to

- store and clear values from the browser's local storage;

- run queries programmatically;

- open or close modal windows;

- navigate to different pages in your application;

- download files;

- copy text to clipboard; and

- log errors and informational messages to the browser's console.

By utilizing these methods, you get access to a robust platform for building dynamic, data-driven applications that can react to user actions instantly.

In the following sections, we will learn more about the different objects and methods that are part of the Appsmith framework.

The Context Object

The Appsmith Context object is a feature of the Appsmith JavaScript framework that provides information about the current application and user. It is a global variable and can be accessed using the `appsmith` keyword anywhere in your application. Its structure is like this:

```
{
    "user": {
        "email": "<logged_in_user_email>",
        "username": "<logged_in_username>",
        "enableTelemetry": false,
        "idToken": {},
        "accountNonExpired": true,
        "accountNonLocked": true,
        "credentialsNonExpired": true,
        "emptyInstance": false,
        "isAnonymous": false,
        "isEnabled": true,
        "isSuperUser": false,
        "isConfigurable": true,
        "adminSettingsVisible": false
    },
    "URL": {
        "fullPath": "http://localhost/app/retroreels/
        login-page-64a1af316c7d33394d1797ba/edit",
```

```
            "host": "localhost",
            "hostname": "localhost",
            "queryParams": {},
            "protocol": "http:",
            "pathname": "/app/retroreels/login-
            page-64a1af316c7d33394d1797ba/edit",
            "port": "",
            "hash": ""
    },
    "store": {},
    "geolocation": {
            "canBeRequested": true,
            "currentPosition": {}
    },
    "mode": "EDIT",
    "theme": {
            "colors": {
                    "primaryColor": "#553DE9",
                    "backgroundColor": "#F8FAFC"
            },
            "borderRadius": {
                    "appBorderRadius": "0.375rem"
            },
            "boxShadow": {
                    "appBoxShadow": "0 1px 3px 0 rgba(0, 0, 0,
                    0.1), 0 1px 2px 0 rgba(0, 0, 0, 0.06)"
            },
            "fontFamily": {
            "appFont": "Nunito Sans"
            }
    }
}
```

As you can see, the Context object provides a wealth of information about the application and the currently logged-in user. You can access the email address and the username of the user, the current page's URL and associated information, the mode your application is currently in (VIEW or EDIT), and the currently applied theme.

You can use the dot notation to access different fields of the Context object:

```
{{ const host = appsmith.URL.host; }}
```

The Query Object

Appsmith's Query JavaScript object is a critical part of the platform's functionality, offering you a flexible and powerful tool to manage data queries of the respective applications. It primarily facilitates the creation, execution, and management of SQL or NoSQL database queries. Appsmith's Query object is not only simple to use, but also greatly reduces the amount of boilerplate code you need to write, thereby speeding up the overall development process.

You worked with Appsmith's Query object in the previous chapter, although we did not introduce the "object" part of its behavior then. Every query you created in Chapter 3 is actually a separate Query object, which contains its own properties and methods. This allows you to run your queries programmatically, as well as access its data, even if it is not bound to a specific widget.

The structure of a Query object looks like this:

```
{
    "actionId": "6497119788e5c93e957fca2d",
    "data": [
        {
            "customer_id": 582,
            "store_id": 2,
```

```
                "first_name": "ANDY",
                "last_name": "VANHORN",
                "email": "ANDY.VANHORN@sakilacustomer.org",
                "address_id": 588,
                "active": true,
                "create_date": "2006-02-14T22:04:37Z",
                "last_update": "2006-02-15T04:57:20Z"
            }
        ],
        "isLoading": false,
        "responseMeta": {
            "isExecutionSuccess": true
        },
        "config": {
            "timeoutInMillisecond": 10000,
            "paginationType": "NONE",
            "encodeParamsToggle": true,
            "body": {
            "value": "select * from customer where email =
            $email",
                "parameters": {
                    "email": "ANDY.VANHORN@
                    sakilacustomer.org"
                }
            }
        }
}
```

It consists of several key parts:

- `actionId`: This is a unique identifier for the query, which is used by Appsmith internally.

- `data`: This object contains the results of the query execution, and is updated every time the query is run. The current state of the object contains data from the *last successful execution* of the query.

- `isLoading`: This Boolean value indicates if the query is currently executing. It's helpful for managing the UI state, like showing a loading spinner.

- `responseMeta`: This contains the metadata from the last successful execution of the query.

- `config`: This object contains the configuration of the query to be executed, including its timeouts, pagination details, and the actual query with its parameters.

- `error`: This will contain any error message if the query fails.

Furthermore, the Query object also defines two methods to control its execution:

- **run()**: As the name suggests, `run()` is used to run a particular Query object. In case the query runs successfully, its output is put into the data field of the object.

- **clear()**: This method is used to clear the results of the previous execution from the data attribute of the Query object. This is especially useful when you want to ensure that old data doesn't interfere with new data or when you want to reset the state of your application.

Parameters for the Query Object

Most SQL queries are not static. They expect parameter values to be substituted at runtime. In the previous section, for example, look at `query. config.body.value`. It contains the following query:

```
select * from customer where email = $email
```

In this case, we need to supply the value of the `$email` parameter at runtime. To facilitate this, the `run()` method of the Query object takes an object as input:

```
query.run({email: "ANDY.VANHORN@sakilacustomer.org"})
```

And while defining the query, you can refer to the parameters like this:

```
select * from customer where email = {{this.params.email}}
```

Synchronous and Asynchronous JavaScript

When developing applications in Appsmith, you'll often interact with JavaScript methods that are asynchronous (async) or synchronous (sync). Understanding the difference between these two types of methods is vital to the performance and functionality of your applications.

JavaScript is single-threaded, meaning it can only perform one operation at a time. Sync methods are executed sequentially, blocking the execution thread until they are completed. This might be fine for simple, quick operations, but for tasks that take longer to execute (like network requests, file operations, or database queries), using sync methods can lead to an unresponsive or slow application. This is where async methods come in.

Async methods are non-blocking; they allow JavaScript to continue executing other code while the async operation is being processed. When the async operation is completed, a callback function is executed to handle the result. In JavaScript, async functions usually return a promise, which is an object that represents the eventual completion (or failure) of an asynchronous operation and its resulting value.

Appsmith provides a variety of widgets, each with different properties, to help developers design intuitive and efficient user interfaces. Understanding when and where to use sync and async methods with these widget properties is crucial for a smooth and responsive app experience.

Most widget properties in Appsmith can work with sync methods, as they typically deal with instant operations. For example, the properties related to a widget's appearance, like isVisible, text, image, borderRadius, and backgroundColor, all work synchronously. If you want to change the text in a Text widget or the visibility of a Button widget based on user interaction or some other condition, these changes happen instantly and synchronously.

Meanwhile, widget properties that deal with data fetched from a database or an API must be handled asynchronously. This is because these operations involve latency due to network requests, and they can't be completed instantly. Good examples of properties that might need async methods include tableData, any options for a Dropdown widget, or the defaultOptionValue for a Select widget.

A typical example of this is when you want to populate a Table widget with data from a database query. In Appsmith, the run() method of the Query object is an async function. It returns a promise, which means you can use it with the await keyword within an async function to pause the execution until the promise is resolved or rejected.

Three Ways to Write Asynchronous JavaScript

There are primarily three different ways to write asynchronous JavaScript: callbacks, promises, and async/await. To explain these paradigms, let us take a single example and write it in each of these ways.

Assume that we need to call three queries: Query1, Query2, and Query3. The result of Query1 is to be used as an input to Query2, whose result, in turn, is to be used as an input to Query3. We will show the result of Query3 as an alert in Appsmith.

Callbacks

A callback function is a function passed into another function as an argument, which is then invoked inside the outer function. This is the fundamental way that JavaScript handles asynchronous operations. However, callbacks can lead to code that is hard to read and maintain, especially when you have multiple nested callbacks, often referred to as "callback hell."

The basic syntax of a callback method is like this:

```
SomeObject.method(
    () => {}, // callback on success
    () => {}, // callback on failure
    {} // input parameters for the method
)
```

With this structure in place, we can rewrite our problem statement:

1. Run Query1 and store its response in response1.

2. If Query1 is successful, run Query2 with response1 as input, and store its response in response2.

3. If Query2 is successful, run Query3 with response2 as input, and store its response in response3.

4. If Query3 is successful, show an alert with the contents of resposne3.

Let's build this step by step.

Step 1: Run Query1.

```
executeQueries: () => {
    return Query1.run(() => {}, () => {}, {input: 'Ran
    Query 1 '})
}
```

Step 2: Run Query2 on successful completion of Query1:

```
executeQueries: () => {
    return Query1.run((response1) => {
        Query2.run(() => {}, () => {}, {input: response1 +
        'Ran Query 2 '})
    }, () => {}, {input: 'Ran Query 1 '})
}
```

Step 3: Run Query3 on successful completion of Query2:

```
executeQueries: () => {
    return Query1.run((response1) => {
        Query2.run((response2) => {
            Query3.run(() => {}, () => {}, {input:
            response2 + 'Ran Query 3'})
        }, () => {}, {input: response1 + 'Ran Query 2 '})
    }, () => {}, {input: 'Ran Query 1 '})
}
```

Step 4: Show an alert on successful completion of Query3:

```
executeQueries: () => {
    return Query1.run((response1) => {
        Query2.run((response2) => {
            Query3.run((response3) => {
                showAlert(response3)
            }, () => {}, {input: response2 + 'Ran
            Query 3'})
```

```
        }, () => {}, {input: response1 + 'Ran Query 2 '})
    }, () => {}, {input: 'Ran Query 1 '})
}
```

As you can see, even a simple requirement of running three queries one after the other has resulted in a difficult-to-read code snippet, and this is *without* handling any errors. Imagine the complexity then!

Promises

A promise is a JavaScript object that links the "producing code" and the "consuming code" together. In other words, this is a container for an asynchronously delivered value. A promise is in one of three states: pending (initial state, neither fulfilled nor rejected), fulfilled (meaning that the operation completed successfully), or rejected (meaning that the operation failed).

Promises are designed to solve the problems of "callback hell" and "inversion of control." They provide a clear, flexible way for functions to return asynchronous values. Promises can be chained together and will propagate results down the chain. They provide two methods: then() for handling successful completion, and catch() for handling errors.

The same example of running three queries one after the other can be written using promises like this:

```
executeQueries: () => {
    return Query1.run({input: 'Ran Query 1 '})
        .then(response => Query2.run({input: response +
        'Ran Query 2 '}))
        .then(response => Query3.run({input: response +
        'Ran Query 3 '}))
        .then(response => showAlert(response))
        .catch(e => showAlert(e.message))
}
```

You immediately notice that the code snippet using promises is much more readable than the one using callback methods. Moreover, you can use a *single* catch() method to handle all exceptions in the entire chain, unlike the callback methods, where you would have had to handle errors individually for each of the three query methods.

async / await

This is a new way to write asynchronous code that is built on top of promises. It is essentially syntactic sugar over promises, making asynchronous code look and behave more like synchronous code, which makes it easier to understand and write. An async function is a function that implicitly returns a promise, and the await keyword is used inside an async function to pause the execution of the function until a promise is resolved or rejected.

Here's the code snippet that runs three queries, one after another, using the async/await mechanism:

```
executeQueries: async () => {
    try {
        let response = await Query1.run({input: 'Ran
        Query 1 '});
        response = await Query2.run({input: response + 'Ran
        Query 2 '});
        response = await Query3.run({input: response + 'Ran
        Query 3 '});
        showAlert(response);
    } catch (e) {
        showAlert(e.message);
    }
}
```

Using the async/await mechanism, you can write traditional JavaScript without resorting to any exotic syntax, and use the standard `try..catch` blocks to handle errors.

Each of these methods for handling asynchronous operations in JavaScript has its place. Callbacks are basic and compatible with all browsers, but can lead to complex and hard-to-read code. Promises help solve this issue, providing a more robust way to handle asynchronous operations, but can still become complex with complex operations. Lastly, async/await simplifies handling promises, making your asynchronous code cleaner and easier to read and reason through.

Programmatically Controlling Appsmith Widgets

Appsmith is designed with the philosophy that developers should be empowered to tailor user interfaces and workflows to their precise needs. To facilitate this, Appsmith supports a range of actions that you can perform programmatically on widgets using JavaScript. This means you can control and manipulate widgets' behavior based on the application's state, user input, or any other dynamic condition that JavaScript can evaluate.

Throughout this section, we'll dive into various scenarios demonstrating how you can enhance the interactivity of your app. From storing values in the browser's local storage for persisting state across sessions, to opening and closing modals to guide the user flow, presenting alerts to give users feedback, and even allowing file downloads — you'll learn how to make your Appsmith application more interactive and responsive.

Let's briefly introduce the scope and utility of these actions.

Store Value

This action allows you to store data in the browser's local storage. It's a handy tool when you want to persist some piece of data across different pages or even different sessions; for instance, user preferences or a shopping cart's state.

Appsmith provides a number of methods to interact with the localStorage object, as detailed in Table 4-1.

Table 4-1. *AppSmith Methods to Interact with localStorage*

Method	Signature	Parameters
storeValue	storeValue(key: string, value: any, persist? = true)	**key**: Name of the key to be added/updated **value**: The data you need to save **persist**: Whether to persist the data across page loads. Defaults to true.
removeValue	removeValue(key: string)	**key: Name of the key to be removed**
clearStore	clearStore()	**Removes all key–value pairs from the** localStorage

You can access the values stored in localStorage via the appsmith. store object:

```
{{ const value = appsmith.store.key }}
```

It's important to note that while localStorage is convenient and widely supported, it is a synchronous API and can block the main thread, which might lead to performance issues. Also, it's not designed to store sensitive data as it has no form of data protection or encryption. Moreover, its data is vulnerable to cross-site scripting (XSS) attacks, so you need to be careful about what data you put into the localStorage object.

Security issues notwithstanding, the appsmith.store object provides a convenient way to persist the global state for your application.

Navigate To

Programmatically navigating between pages in your Appsmith app becomes a breeze with the Navigate To action. It allows you to redirect users to different pages or external URLs based on specific conditions or actions, like a successful form submission.

The navigateTo method takes the following arguments:

pageNameOrUrl

Specifies the page name (for internal navigation) or the URL (for external navigation). For example, to navigate to an external URL:

```
navigateTo("https://google.com")
```

and to another page in your Appsmith app:

```
navigateTo("CustomerDashboard")
```

assuming that a page called ConsumerDashboard exists in your application. Note that page names are case sensitive.

params (optional)

Specifies an object containing parameters sent to the page during navigation. For example, if you want to pass a variable, say, the preferred language of the user as a parameter, you can call the navigateTo method like this:

```
{{navigateTo("CustomerDashboard", {"lang": "en-us"})}}
```

This parameter can then be accessed on the target page using the Context object:

```
const language = appsmith.URL.queryParams.lang;
```

target (optional)

Specifies whether the target page should be opened in a new window (NEW_WINDOW) or not (SAME_WINDOW). By default, all navigations happen on the same window.

Here's an example of a navigateTo() method call with all parameters included:

```
{{navigateTo("CustomerDashboard", {"lang": "en-us"},
"NEW_WINDOW")}}
```

Show Alert

Alerts are a great way to give instant feedback or important information to your users. The Show Alert action lets you trigger alerts programmatically, giving you the flexibility to customize the message and its timing.

The showAlert() method takes two arguments: message and style (optional), where style can be one of:

- success

- info

- warning

- error

Here's an example of the showAlert() method in action:

```
showAlert("This is a successful alert.", "success");
showAlert("This is an informational alert.", "info");
showAlert("This alert is here to warn you.", "warning");
showAlert("Alert, something is broken!", "error");
```

Show / Close Modals

Modals are instrumental in managing user flows, drawing attention to critical information, or collecting user input. With Show Modal and Close Modal, you can control when a modal appears and disappears, based on user interaction or any other condition evaluated by your JavaScript code.

Both showModal() and closeModal() methods take a single argument - the name of the Modal widget to be shown / closed. You need to make sure a Modal widget with the same name (case sensitive) is present on your page before triggering this action.

```
showModal("UpdateCustomerModal");
closeModal("UpdateCustomerModal");
```

Download

This action enables your users to download files directly from your Appsmith app. Whether it's generating and downloading a report or allowing users to download user manuals, the Download action serves a wide range of purposes.

The signature of the function looks like this:

```
download(data: any, fileName: string, fileType?: string)
```

Let's break down its parameters:

1. **data (any):** This is the content that you want to include in the downloaded file. It can be any data type — from simple text, numbers, to complex data structures like arrays or objects.

2. **fileName (string):** This parameter determines the name of the file as it will be saved on the user's machine. It should be a string and does not include the file extension.

3. **fileType (string, optional)**: This is an optional
   parameter that denotes the file's format or extension
   (like 'txt', 'csv', 'json', etc.). If not specified, the
   function defaults to creating a text file.

Now, consider a use case where you might want to provide your users
with the ability to download a report, represented as a JSON object:

```
const data = {
    "Report": "Q1 Earnings",
    "Revenue": "$200,000",
    "Profit": "$150,000"
};
const fileName = "Q1_Earnings_Report";
const fileType = "json";

download(data, fileName, fileType);
```

In the above code, the download function will trigger a download of a
JSON file named "Q1_Earnings_Report.json" with the specified report data.

One critical aspect to understand about the download function in
Appsmith is its scope and limitations concerning file type conversions.
The download function, as powerful as it is, does not inherently support
converting data from one file type to another. It merely writes the data
provided to it into a file of the specified type.

For instance, if you pass a JSON object as the data and specify 'csv' as
the file type, the function won't automatically convert the JSON object into
a CSV format. Instead, it would write the JSON string directly into a CSV
file, which is unlikely to be the desired outcome.

Therefore, if you need to convert data from one format to another
(like from JSON to CSV, or vice versa), you'll need to perform this
conversion explicitly using JavaScript before passing the data to the
download function. There are numerous libraries and functions available
in JavaScript for these conversions, and you would need to utilize them
depending on your specific use case.

Here's an example of how you might convert a JSON object to CSV format using a simple custom function before downloading it:

```
function convertToCSV(objArray) {
    const array = typeof objArray !== 'object' ? JSON.
    parse(objArray) : objArray;
    let str = `${Object.keys(array[0]).join()},\r\n`;

    return array.reduce((str, next) => {
        str += `${Object.values(next).join()},\r\n`;
        return str;
        }, str);
}

const data = [
    { "name": "John Doe", "email": "john.doe@example.com" },
    { "name": "Jane Doe", "email": "jane.doe@example.com" }
];
const csvData = convertToCSV(data);
const fileName = "user_info";
const fileType = "csv";

download(csvData, fileName, fileType);
```

In addition to the above, Appsmith also provides the following minor functionalities as part of its Javascript framework:

Copy to Clipboard: Sometimes, you might want to allow your users to copy some information quickly. The Copy to Clipboard action provides this functionality, letting users copy text to their clipboard with a single button click.

```
copyToClipboard(data: string, options: object)
```

Reset Widget: Resetting a widget to its initial state is often needed, especially in forms where you might want to clear the inputs after a successful submission. Reset Widget does just that, restoring the widget to its initial state.

```
resetWidget(widgetName: string, resetChildren?: boolean = true)
```

Set Interval and Clear Interval: These actions provide control over repeated execution of a piece of code at specific time intervals. With Set Interval, you can start this timed repetition, while Clear Interval allows you to stop it when the condition is met or the task is completed.

```
setInterval(callbackFunction: Function, interval: number, id?:
string, args?: any)
clearInterval(id: string)
```

By now, you've amassed a robust understanding of the JavaScript-related functionalities of Appsmith. You've ventured into the realms of Query and Console objects, navigated through synchronous and asynchronous methods, explored the depths of callbacks, promises, and async/await, and even harnessed the power of controlling widget actions programmatically. Your toolkit is brimming with knowledge about how to work with data, perform various actions, manipulate widgets, and even handle files with JavaScript in Appsmith.

But the real strength of this knowledge can only be fully appreciated when applied in the context of a real-world application. So, now it's time to roll up your sleeves and put your newfound skills into practice. In the next section of our book, we're going to guide you through the exciting journey of creating a multi-page application using Appsmith. You'll be able to observe, first-hand, how all these JavaScript capabilities blend seamlessly into building practical, functional, and interactive applications. Let's embark on this adventure and unlock the true potential of low-code development with Appsmith.

Introducing RetroReels

Welcome to RetroReels, a fascinating foray into the past where the charm of cinema thrives in its physical form. RetroReels is our fictitious DVD rental store and the centerpiece for this chapter's multi-page Appsmith application.

Our multi-page application will emulate the real-world operations of RetroReels. It will allow us to manage the extensive film inventory, keep track of customer transactions, monitor rental and return dates, and provide analytical reports for the store's performance.

Through this section, we will develop an application that streamlines the operations of RetroReels and helps the store maintain its extensive catalogue and customer interactions smoothly. This will provide us with a practical and comprehensive understanding of how to create complex application flows in Appsmith.

High level design

The RetroReels app will allow two type of users to log in:

- **Customer:** A customer is a member of the general public who wants to browse DVDs (or search for their favorite one), and manage their own rentals. They would be able to rent new DVDs, view the titles they're currently renting, and return the ones that they have finished watching.

- **Staff Member:** A Staff Member is employed by RetroReels whose job is to manage inventory. After logging in, they would be able to Add/Remove titles from RetroReels's collection, and view/download Rental Reports.

Here's the use-case diagram for the proposed application:

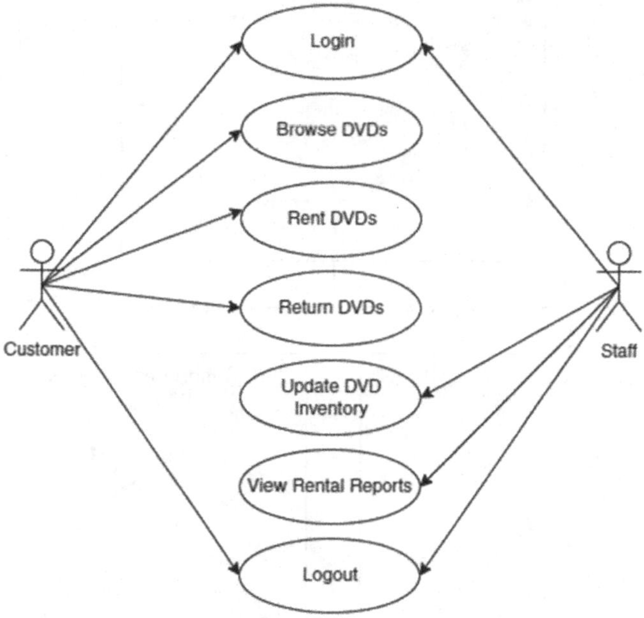

Figure 4-4. *Use-case diagram for RetroReels Application*

Users, depending on whether they log in as a Customer or a Staff Member, will be redirected to a different screen post login, where they will be able to perform actions enabled for their roles. We will, therefore, create three screens (or *pages*, in Appsmith parlance) in the application. One corresponding to the login screen, and two others corresponding to the Customer dashboard and the Staff dashboard, respectively.

The following figure shows the proposed navigation. Upon logout, both Customer and Staff Dashboard will redirect the user back to the Login screen.

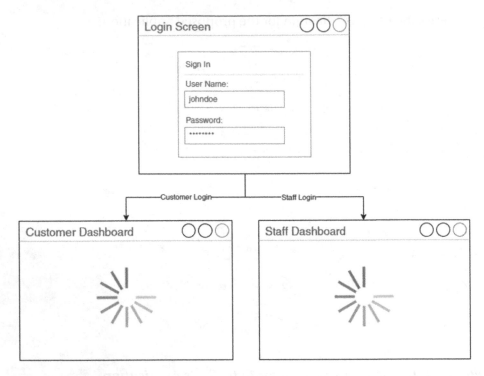

Figure 4-5. *Proposed screens for the RetroReels Application*

The Login Page

The Login Page is going to be the entry point of our application. Upon launching the app, the user will be given an option to either log in as a *Customer* or as a *Staff Member*. If they're able to provide the correct credentials, the user will be redirected to the correct dashboard, otherwise an error message will be displayed on screen.

In order to start building this, you need to create a new Application in Appsmith. To do so, log in to your Appsmith instance and click on the + **New** button on the top-right corner. You will be redirected immediately to the canvas editor of a newly created application. Go ahead, and rename the application to RetroReels.

Unlike the examples in the previous chapters, the RetroReels app will be a multi-page application. The first page of the app ("Page1"), should already be created in your new app. Change its name to "Login Page" by clicking on the three-dot menu[3] next to its name and choosing the Edit Name option.

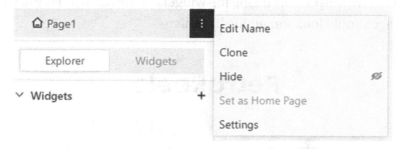

Figure 4-6. *Editing a page's name*

For defining the page's structure, we will use the following widgets:

- **Tabs Widget**: This widget lets you organize related content into separate tabs, thereby reducing the cognitive load on the user. We will use the Tabs widget to provide separate login forms for Customers and Staff Members

- **Container Widget**: This widget acts as a wrapper that can hold and group other widgets together, and provides a convenient way to manage the visual hierarchy of your application.

- **JSON Form Widget**: The JSON Form widget makes creating complex forms much easier by typing a bit of JSON, rather than dragging-and-dropping multiple widgets on the Canvas editor. We will use it to create login forms for the Customers and Staff Members.

---

[3] The three-dot menu only appears when you hover over the page name

To create the Login page structure, first place the Container widget in the center of the Canvas Editor, and then overlay the Tabs widget over it. Use the right sidebar on the Tabs widget to create two tabs, one each for the Customer and the Staff login. Afterwards, add a JSON Form widget to each of the tabs, with each form having a Username and a Password field. Once you have finished arranging the widgets on the Canvas Editor, your Login page should look something like this:

Figure 4-7. *The completed Login page*

Adding the Login Functionality

Now that we have successfully finalized the design of our Login screen, the next step is implementing the much-anticipated login functionality, so that customers and staff members can log in to their respective dashboards and start interacting with RetroReels.

To build this, we are going to take the following approach:

1. Get the username (Email) and password input from the user.

2. Look up the details in the respective database table.

3. If the details match, navigate the user to either the Customer or the Staff dashboard, depending on which login form was used.

4. In case the details do not match, show an error on the screen.

Before we go any further though, we need to create two placeholder pages (one each for the Customer and the Staff dashboard) in our app, so that we can define the targets for navigation. Go ahead and create two new pages in the application, and name them `CustomerDashboard` and `StaffDashboard` respectively. For now, put a text widget on each of those pages, identifying them. We will fill them up with appropriate content in the later sections.

With the placeholder pages in place, it is time to start writing the queries and Javascript objects to develop the Login functionality.

Firstly, we will create **two** SQL queries, one each for the `customer` and `staff` tables in the Sakila database. Use the left sidebar to create these two queries, and name them `CustDetails` and `StaffDetails` respectively:

```
SELECT * FROM customer WHERE email = {{this.params.email}}
SELECT * FROM staff WHERE email = {{this.params.email}}
```

Next, let's write the login methods for Customer and Staff. To begin, create a new JS object from the left sidebar and call it LoginObject. Create a custLogin method inside it as follows:

```
custLogin: async (input) => {
    let customer = await CustDetails.run(input);
    if (customer.length > 0) {
        storeValue("customer", customer[0]);
        navigateTo("CustomerDashboard");
    }
    else {
        showAlert("Could not find user", 'error');
    }
}
```

This simple method above runs the CustDetails query that we just created asynchronously. If a customer with matching email was found, the method stores the customer object in the browser's localStorage, and navigates the user to the CustomerDashboard page. Otherwise, an alert is shown on the screen saying that the particular user was not found.

We're now ready to bind this method to the Customer Login button. To do this, find the CustLoginForm widget on the Canvas editor, and bind the following code to its onSubmit action[4]:

```
{{LoginObject.custLogin({email: CustLoginForm.formData.
email})}}
```

---

[4] You will have to click on the little JS button present alongside onSubmit to enable the textbox.

The above piece of code tells Appsmith to call the custLogin method located inside LoginObject JS object, and as an input to the method, send a key called email, with its value populated with whatever was added by the user in the email field of the CustLoginForm widget.

And that's it! You have successfully completed the Customer Login functionality of the RetroReels app. To test it out, put the app in Preview mode, open the Login page, add any random email in the input box, and click on submit. Most probably, that email ID does not exist in the customer table of the Sakila database, so you would see an error on your screen.

Next, open the customer table using your favorite DB editor, and copy an email address contained in it. Upon submitting this particular email ID in the Login form, you will find that Appsmith has redirected you to the CustomerDashboard page.

Caution   *What about passwords?*

You will notice that we haven't made use of the Password field during the login process. This is because customer passwords are not maintained in the Sakila sample database. You should **never** do this with your production database.

We talk more about authentication and authorization mechanisms in Appsmith in Chapter 8.

Now that you have set up Customer login, you can follow the same process to set up Staff login as well. This is left as an exercise to the reader.

The Customer Dashboard

Once a Customer logs in inside the RetroReels app, they are able to perform the following actions:

- View a list of available films that they can rent, and rent any of those.

- View a list of films they have currently rented, and return any of those.

- Log out of the application.

This means that we need to write the following queries and methods:

- A query to return a list of all films available to rent.

- A query to return a list of all films that the logged in user has rented.

- A method to rent a particular film.

- A method to return a particular film.

- A method for the user to log out of the application.

Also, to the very least, we would require the following widgets on the CustomerDashboard page:

- A main container which will house all other widgets.

- A title widget (copied over from the Login page).

- A text widget displaying the name of the currently logged in user.

- A button widget for the user to log out.

- A table widget for displaying all the available films.

- A table widget for displaying all the currently rented films.

- A button widget each for renting and returning films.

Drag these widgets on the Canvas editor and create a page resembling something like below. It's okay if your widgets don't show any data yet, we'll get it to show in the later sections.

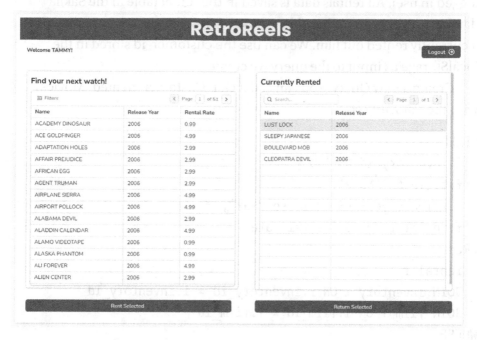

Figure 4-8. *The Customer Dashboard*

Fetching Data

The first thing that we need to show on screen is the name of the currently logged in user! If you remember, in the previous section we had saved the Customer details in the browser's localStorage upon successful login. We can now make use of Appsmith's store object to read those details. Bind the following code to the text widget welcoming the user:

```
Welcome {{appsmith.store.customer.first_name}}!
```

Getting the currently rented films

Next, let's work on getting the data on the currently rented films of the logged in user. All rentals data is saved in the rental table in the Sakila database. Every row in the table, whose return_date is NULL, represents a currently rented out film. We can use the customer_id stored in the localStorage as input to the query we create.

Create a new Query (you can call it Get_Customer_Rented_Movies) with the following code:

```
SELECT
  i.inventory_id AS 'ID',
  f.title AS 'Name',
  f.release_year AS 'Release Year',
  f.rental_rate AS 'Rental Rate'
FROM
  rental r
  JOIN inventory i ON r.inventory_id = i.inventory_id
  JOIN film f ON i.film_id = f.film_id
WHERE
  customer_id = {{appsmith.store.customer.customer_id}}
  AND return_date <=> NULL
```

While you are creating this query, go to its Settings, and turn on the "Run query on page load" option. This will make sure that the data is available for the customer to view as soon as the dashboard is loaded. Also, this can now be easily bound to the Rented Movies table.

Getting the films available to rent

We can take the following approach to figure out which movies are available to rent on RetroReels:

- The universe of movies in RetroReels inventory can be found in the inventory table. We can use a group by clause to know how many copies of each movie are available.

- All the movies currently rented out can be found in the rentals table. Here too, we can use the group by clause to know how many copies of each movie are currently rented out.

- By subtracting the rented out movies from the available ones, we can figure out which films can be rented out today.

The query that accomplishes all this is given below:

```
SELECT
  added.film_id as 'ID',
  added.title as 'Name',
  added.release_year as 'Release Year',
  added.rental_rate as 'Rental Rate'
FROM
  (
    SELECT
      COUNT(i.inventory_id) AS num_added,
      f.title,
      f.film_id,
      f.release_year,
      f.rental_rate
```

```
    FROM
      inventory i
      JOIN film f ON i.film_id = f.film_id
    GROUP BY
      i.film_id
  ) AS added
  LEFT JOIN (
    SELECT
      COUNT(r.inventory_id) AS num_rented,
      f.title,
      f.film_id
    FROM
      rental r
      JOIN inventory i ON r.inventory_id = i.inventory_id
      JOIN film f ON i.film_id = f.film_id
    WHERE
      r.return_date <=> NULL
    GROUP BY
      i.film_id
  ) AS rented ON added.film_id = rented.film_id
WHERE
  (
    num_added - IF (
      rented.num_rented <=> NULL, 0, rented.num_rented
    )
  ) > 0
LIMIT {{ AvailableMoviesTable.pageSize }}
OFFSET {{ AvailableMoviesTable.pageOffset }};
```

As you can see, we have implemented Server-Side pagination in this query. To bind it correctly to the table, we also need to create a Count query. Creating this query is as simple as:

```
SELECT COUNT(*) FROM (<Insert Available Films Query Here>);
```

Create both these queries (call them Available_Movies and Available_Movies_Count respectively), and bind it to the AvailableMoviesTable as follows:

- **Table Data**: {{Available_Movies.data}}

- **Server Side Pagination**: true

- **Total Records**: {{Available_Movies_Count.data[0]. available}}

- **On Page Change**: {{Available_Movies.run()}}

Renting and Returning films

The customer should be able to rent any of the available films in the RetroReels catalogue, as well as return films that they are currently renting from the platform. To rent a new movie, the customer would:

- Select a row from the Available Films table

- Click on the "Rent Selected" button

- The film would then be rented against their Customer ID and start showing up in the Currently Rented table

Similarly, to return a film, the customer would:

- Select a row from the Currently Rented table

- Click on the "Return Selected" button

- The film would then be returned and would vanish from the Currently Rented table.

A set of simple SQL queries and JS methods can accomplish this functionality, whose listing is given below.

Query: Get_Inventory_Id

```
SELECT
  MAX(i.inventory_id) AS inventory_id
FROM
  inventory i
  JOIN rental r ON i.inventory_id = r.inventory_id
WHERE
  i.film_id = {{this.params.film_id}}
  AND r.return_date IS NOT NULL
```

Query: Insert_Rental

```
INSERT INTO rental(
  rental_date, inventory_id, customer_id,
  staff_id
)
VALUES
  (
    NOW(), {{this.params.inventory_id}},
    {{appsmith.store.customer.customer_id}}, 1
  );
```

Query: Return_Rental

```
UPDATE
  rental
SET
  return_date = NOW()
WHERE
  customer_id = {{appsmith.store.customer.customer_id}}
  AND inventory_id = {{this.params.inventory_id}}
  AND return_date <=> NULL;
```

JS Method: **rentMovie**

```
async rentMovie(input) {
    let inventory = await Get_Inventory_Id.run({film_id:
    input.film_id});
    if (inventory.length > 0) {
        let rental = await Insert_Rental.run({inventory_id:
        inventory[0].inventory_id});
        await Get_Customer_Rented_Movies.run();
    }
    else {
        showAlert("Movie is not available to rent.",
        "error");
    }
}
```

JS Method: **returnMovie**

```
async returnMovie(input) {
    await Return_Rental.run({inventory_id: input.
    inventory_id});
    await Get_Customer_Rented_Movies.run();
}
```

JS Method: **logout**

```
async logout() {
    clearStore();
    navigateTo("Login");
}
```

The methods rentMovie(), returnMovie(), and logout() should be bound to the "Rent Selected", "Return Selected", and the "Logout" button respectively, with the following code:

Rent Selected

```
{{CustomerMethods.rentMovie({film_id: AvailableMoviesTable.
selectedRow.ID})}}
```

Return Selected

```
{{CustomerMethods.returnMovie({inventory_id: RentedMoviesTable.
selectedRow.inventory_id})}}
```

Logout

```
{{CustomerMethods.logout()}}
```

This assumes that the name of the JS object in CustomerDashboard is called CustomerMethods.

Once you have created these queries and JS objects, and bound them to the appropriate widget, *your Customer Dashboard should be ready!.* You should now be able to log in to RetroReels as a customer, and rent and return movies to your heart's content. Furthermore, you should also see appropriate entries being made in the rental table in accordance to your actions on the GUI.

The Staff Dashboard

As a Staff Member of RetroReels, you should be able to log into the application and be redirected to a staff-only area. Once there, you should be able to view all the rentals that happened today, as well as update the inventory of any film part of the RetroReels catalogue.

It is a simple dashboard that looks like this:

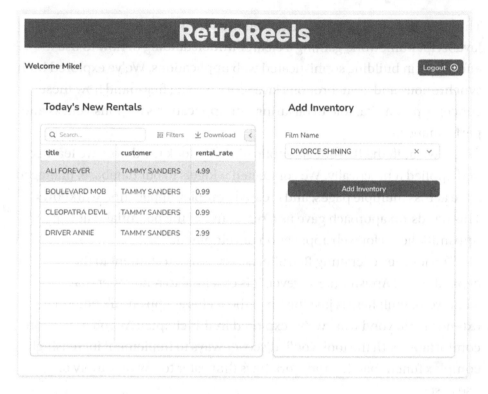

Figure 4-9. *The Staff Dashboard*

You will find many elements from the Customer Dashboard also present here, like the Text widget displaying the logged in user's name, the Logout button, as well as a table widget showing a list of films (albeit the ones that got rented out today).

As you have followed along the chapter and created the Login page and the Customer Dashboard page, you should now be confident enough to figure out the widgets needed to create the UI presented above, as well as the queries and JS methods to make it work. You are advised to create the Staff Dashboard on your own, using the knowledge you have gained by reading this chapter.

Summary

Throughout this chapter, we've delved into the intricacies of Appsmith's JavaScript framework, gaining a clearer understanding of how to use it effectively in building sophisticated web applications. We've explored both synchronous and asynchronous JavaScript, seeing first-hand how these concepts play a vital role in ensuring our application's responsiveness and performance.

As we built the RetroReels application, we took the theory we learned and applied it practically. We connected widgets to our database, managed state across multiple pages, and created complex application workflows. This hands-on approach gave us a real sense of the potential that Appsmith holds for web application development.

The journey of crafting RetroReels serves as a testament to the capabilities of Appsmith. However, it is essential to remember that what we've built here is just the tip of the iceberg. Appsmith's potential extends far beyond what we've explored in this chapter. As you grow more comfortable with the tool, you'll discover ways to implement increasingly complex functionalities and workflows that cater to a wide variety of use cases.

As we turn the page on RetroReels, we hope that the experience has fortified your knowledge and confidence in creating complex applications using Appsmith. In the upcoming chapters, we'll delve deeper into other features and functionalities of this powerful tool. Let's continue on this exciting journey, exploring more of what Appsmith has to offer, and discovering how to leverage it to its fullest potential.

CHAPTER 5

Integration with Web Services

Today's digital solutions need to deliver several things, like a rich customer experience, optimized business models, multiple channels to market, and more. The organization's digital landscape has individual components offering these new capabilities. These components must integrate to deliver the intended digital innovations. Application programming interfaces (APIs) offer a rapid and easy integration solution based on ubiquitous HTTP data exchange. Low-code development platforms (LCDPs) often support data read and write operations over HTTP protocols like REST and GraphQL.

In the previous chapter, you worked on workflow-based Appsmith applications. In this chapter, you will work with the web service integrations offered in Appsmith. By the end of the chapter, you can be confident working with web services for functions like reading data, updating data, performing actions, fetching status, and so on. These features will enable you to integrate existing solutions to deliver optimized cross-enterprise solutions.

© Rahul Sharma and Rajat Arora 2023
R. Sharma and R. Arora, *Low-Code Development with Appsmith*,
https://doi.org/10.1007/978-1-4842-9813-8_5

Working with GraphQL

In 2015, Facebook introduced GraphQL, a query language that can improve application flexibility, performance, and memory utilization by giving clients precisely the data they request and no more. GraphQL is designed to make APIs fast, flexible, and developer friendly. It allows development teams to add or deprecate fields without impacting existing clients. It also supports pulling data from several sources in a single request rather than requesting from each source individually. In the next section, you will integrate GraphQL to read data. The discussion is limited to the required details only. Complete details about GraphQL and queries are well beyond the scope of this book.

Hands-on: Reminder Notification App

RetroReels is in the movie rental business. Their customers often fail to return movies on time. It leads to missing inventory and monetary losses as outstanding dues. You are tasked to create a Reminder app for internal users. The application should have the following capabilities:

- Determine customers who failed to return titles.

- Send SMS and email notifications to the selected set of users.

GraphQL Setup

RetroReels uses MySQL as its application backend. Direct database access is limited to respective application teams only. Alternatively, the application team has provided a set of GraphQL APIs that can provide the required data. Thus, you must load data using GraphQL APIs for your application use cases.

Several products, both open source and commercial, can be used to enable GraphQL APIs over MySQL. You could also create a small application to accomplish this. Later in this section are the steps to provide a GraphQL API using an open-source tool called Hasura.

Hasura (`https://hasura.io/`) is an open-source product that can auto-generate GraphQL or REST APIs for your data. You are only required to configure your database and specify the data objects. Hasura can capture data model changes and offers a unified REST and GraphQL APIs endpoint. Hasura can also capture data model updates and real-time data updates. The APIs can also support additional authentication for access control. This book does not aim to cover Hasura in detail. Please refer to the product documentation for details.

This section covers the details of exposing a GraphQL API over MySQL. Please refer to Hasura's documentation for more details. MySQL connectivity is offered as an enterprise version trial. As a prerequisite, you need access to an instance of Hasura enterprise version. The following instructions are from Hasura 2.28 enterprise trial version.

Hasura provides deployment guides for various cloud platforms. You can also run Hasura on a workstation using Docker. Please refer to the documentation for more details.

---

1. Open the Hasura Console (Figure 5-1) by navigating to `http://hasura.myhost.com/console`.

Figure 5-1. *Hasura MySQL Connector*

2. From the Console, click the Data tab. Select the MySQL data source driver, enter a display name for the database, and set the JDBC Connection URL for your MySQL instance. The JDBC connection URL should look like `jdbc:mysql://user:password@mysqlhost:3306/sakila`

3. Hasura will be able to fetch all tables in the specified database. Next, you must track tables to generate a full-featured GraphQL API for it automatically. In the preceding problem statement, you need to know the rental details, so make sure to track the same (Figure 5-2).

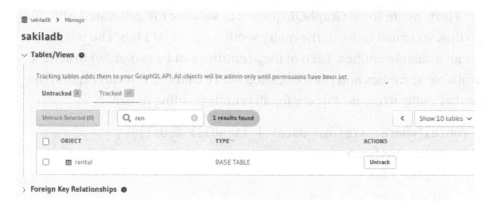

Figure 5-2. *Track tables*

4. Additionally, you must add the required foreign
    key mappings for each table. It will enable Hasura
    to join the two tables and return the attributes of
    the secondary table. Open the Mapping tab of the
    Rentals table and select the available auto-detected
    foreign keys, like `customer_id` and `inventory_id`
    (Figure 5-3). You should repeat the step with the
    Inventory table to fetch the associated film title.

Figure 5-3. *Track foreign keys*

Next, create some GraphQL queries to validate the generated APIs. To do this, you must move to the query section on the API tab. The tab will list all available entities. Each of these entities can be expanded to see the available attributes and the associated where clauses. You can expand the rental entity to create a query for all rentals pending return.

```
{ rental(where: {return_date: {_is_null: true}}) {
    rental_customer {
      first_name
      last_name
      email
    }
    rental_inventory {
      inventory_film {
        title
      } }
    rental_date
  } }
```

The query finds all rental records where return_date is null. The query returns only limited fields, like customer name, email, movie title, and rental date (Figure 5-4).

Figure 5-4. *Hasura Query Editor*

That's all for setting up the GraphQL APIs. Next, you will use the Appsmith framework to read data using these APIs.

GraphQL Queries

Start by creating a new application, named Rental Reminder, in Appsmith. The application will read data using GraphQL queries. Thus, add a new bank GraphQL query by clicking the accordion icon (+) against Queries / JS in the left-hand menu. Create a query named pending_return_api with the following details (Figure 5-5):

- Type: POST, as Hasura provides a POST API

- Endpoint: The location of the Hasura GraphQL engine. You can copy and paste the correct URL from Hasura Console.

151

- Body: Copy the rental entity query created in the previous section. The query fetches all customers where the rental date is null.

Figure 5-5. *GraphQL query*

Lastly, validate the query by clicking the "RUN" button. You should get the entire list of customers as a JSON response. The Query Editor allows you to specify query-specific headers and query parameters/body. By default, all queries have a timeout of 10 seconds, but you can update that from the Settings tab of the Query Editor.

You can render the JSON data in a table for the application users. Thus, add a Table widget to the application editor. You can name it pending_return_list and refer to the previously created pending_return_api for table data (Figure 5-6). The query.data attribute does not contain a list to render table rows. The Hasura JSON response has a data attribute and then a rental sub-attribute. The query.data response field wraps the Hasura JSON response. Thus, update the Table Data field to use the {{pending__return_API.data.data.rental}} expression.

Figure 5-6. *Query response*

As shown, the table is filled with JSON data for customer and film fields. The JSON structure is created from the query provided for execution. This structure is well suited for applications and integration purposes. You can update table columns to display a single attribute of the JSON object (Figure 5-7). Edit the `rental_customer` table column by clicking on the cog icon against it. Update the Column Data field to `{{currentRow["rental_customer"].email}}` value to display customer email in the field. Also, rename the column to `email`. Similarly, update the `rental_inventory` column to display the film title by selecting the `inventory.title` attribute (`{{currentRow["rental_inventory"].inventory_film.title}}`). Rename the column header to `Title`.

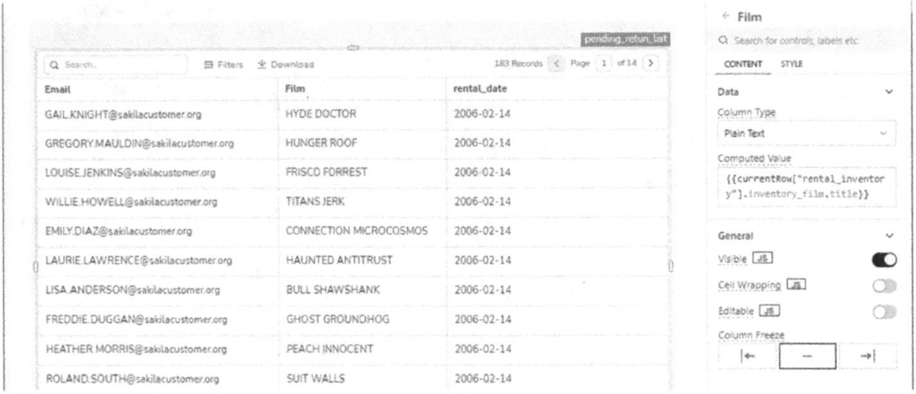

Figure 5-7. *Field selection*

As shown, the table now displays the customer email and film title instead of the JSON data. Customer name details need to be added to it. You should add a column named `first_name` and refer to the `first_name` attribute of the `rental_customer` object (`{{currentRow["rental_customer"].first_name}}`) for table data (Figure 5-8). Similarly, add a new column named `last_name` and refer to the `last_name` attribute of the `rental_customer` object (`{{currentRow["rental_customer"].last_name}}`) for table data.

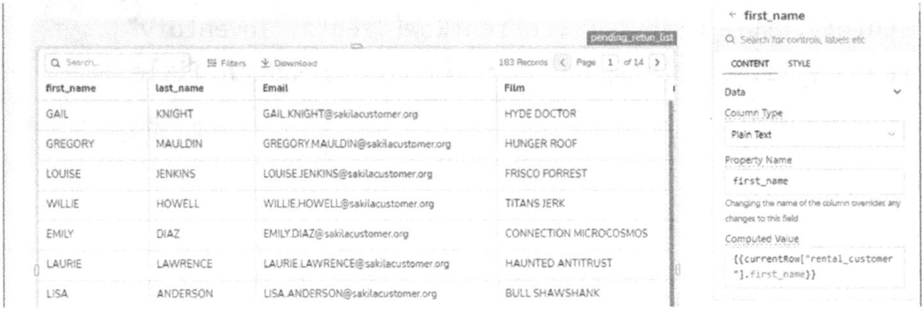

Figure 5-8. *Additional columns*

GraphQL Pagination

The table in the previous section works with JS-based pagination. As discussed in Chapter 3, it is better to work with server-side pagination when working with extensive data. GraphQL supports pagination by using the limit and the offset keywords. You need to update the query to pass these parameters additionally. The pending_return_list table attributes must provide the value for these parameters.

```
{rental(where: {return_date: {_is_null: true}},
    limit: {{pending_return_list.pageSize}},
    offset: {{pending_return_list.pageOffset}}) {
    // Removed for brevity
}}
```

The preceding query binds pending_return_list table widgets pages and page offset properties in the GraphQL queue. Additionally, you need to know the total number of records available. GraphQL supports the concept of aggregation queries for such needs. Aggregate queries fetch consolidated data in various use cases, like count queries that let you count fields satisfying specific criteria or range queries that calculate the maximum, minimum, sum, and average of specified fields. In SQL, a separate query is required to determine the aggregate value. But in GraphQL, update the data query to determine the total count of available data additionally. Please ensure that the aggregate query matches the where clause of the original query, as shown here:

```
{ rental(where: {return_date: {_is_null: true}},
    limit: {{pending_return_list.pageSize}},
    offset: {{pending_return_list.pageOffset}}) {
    // Removed for Brevity
    }
```

```
rental_aggregate(where: {return_date: {_is_null: true}}) {
  aggregate {
    count(distinct: false)
  }
}}
```

This query provides the total number of available records in the `rental_aggregate.aggregate.count` attribute. Thus, update the Total Count field to use the expression to read the count attribute (`{{pending__ return_API.data.data.rental_aggregate.aggregate.count}}`) (Figure 5-9). Lastly, update the `onPageChange` property to specify the query to execute.

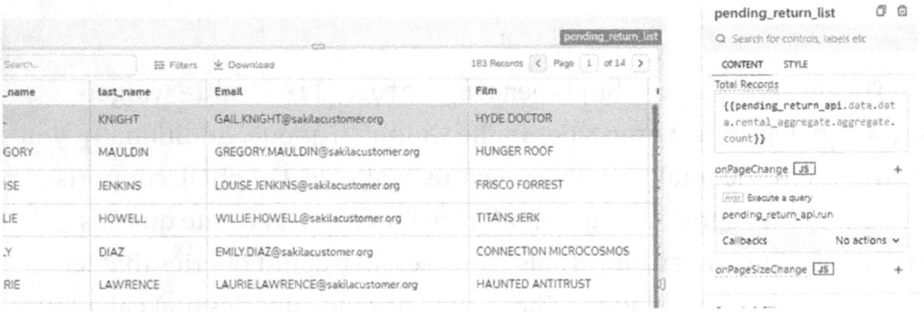

Figure 5-9. *Server-side pagination*

In this section, you read data using GraphQL APIs and displayed it in a table. The APIs are not limited to reading data only. You can also save records using GraphQL APIs. The integration would remain similar to the previous one. So far, you have worked with GraphQL query without its declaration. GraphQL supports creating queries as function definitions, which is beyond the current scope. In such scenarios, the query has a name and arguments (`prefixed with $`) used to configure `where` clause values or pagination values. The Pagination tab on Appsmith Query Editor allows you to bind pagination query arguments to the table-level properties.

```
query fetchRentalPendingCustomers ($pgLimit: Int!,
$pgOffset: Int!){
    rental(where: {return_date: {_is_null: true}}, limit:
    $pgLimit, offset: $pgOffset) {
// Removed for Brevity

  }
}
```

Continuing the problem statement, you need to send reminder notifications to the customers displayed in the list. The following section shows how you can use REST APIs to invoke third-party services to accomplish that.

Working with REST

Today's distributed system architecture integrates over APIs. APIs define a set of rules that specify how different applications can connect to and communicate with each other. Specifically, REST API is an API that conforms to the design principles of the REST, or representational state transfer architectural style. These APIs communicate via HTTP requests to perform standard database functions like creating, reading, updating, and deleting records (also known as CRUD) within a resource. You can use REST-based architecture to support high-performing and reliable communication at scale. You can quickly implement and modify it, bringing visibility and cross-platform portability to any API system. Systems that implement REST APIs can scale efficiently because REST optimizes client–server interactions. They simplify and decouple various server components so that each part can evolve independently. Platform or technology changes at the server application do not affect the client application. You can write both client and server applications in various programming languages without affecting the API design. With so many benefits and flexibility, REST APIs are a de facto standard for integrating applications.

Appsmith provides query connectors, similar to GraphQL, for integrating with REST services. These APIs can be used for reading data, similar to GraphQL integration. As discussed in the following section, you can also use them to perform actions.

Hands-on: Sending Notifications

The RetroReels Reminder app can determine the list of customers with overdue returns. But you have yet to deliver notifications to them. You can send email notifications since the data has a customer email address. Application users should be able to perform the following:

- Select customers and send a reminder with username, film title, and rental date details.

- Users can also provide a specific message for selected customers instead of a generic reminder.

Notifications Service

Notifications, like emails and SMSs, require a service provider capable of delivering these messages at an enterprise scale. These providers offer various features, like dynamic content, capture forms, A/B tracking, notification automation, etc. Several notification providers, like Adobe Campaign, WebEngage, and Mailchimp, are available. The next section showcases integration using the Mailjet notification provider. Thus, it is recommended to create a Mailjet account (`https://app.mailjet.com/signin`). After logging in, please generate API keys from Account ➤ Rest API ➤ API Key Management (Figure 5-10). These keys will be used to authenticate application requests.

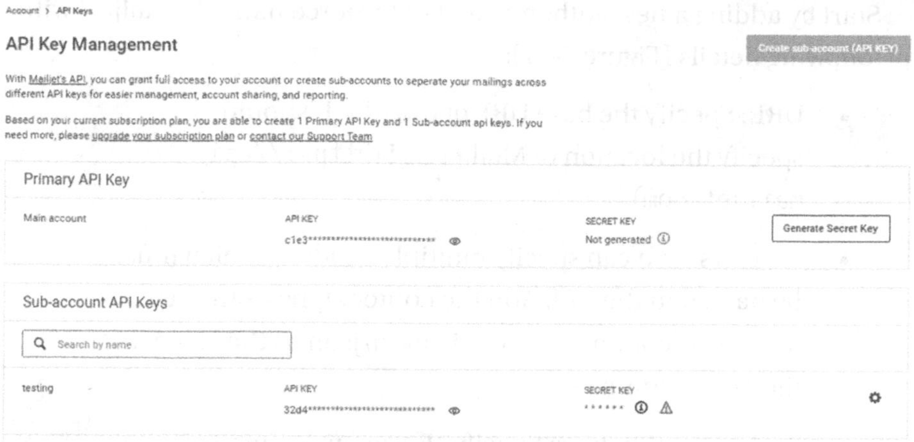

Figure 5-10. *Mailjet API keys*

Authenticated API Datasource

In Chapter 3, you worked with datasources to integrate SQL and NoSQL stores. The datastore configuration asked for DB location, username, password, schema, and other database connection-specific attributes. These attributes govern how Appsmith connects to the specified datasource. Additionally, you added queries to load/save data specified by a datasource.

Appsmith applies the same concept to other components, like REST API and GraphQL. This concept is beneficial when multiple APIs connect to the same service. All these APIs can have common header attributes, like content type, authorization, client name, etc., which can be specified in a datasource. All queries under the datasource will inherit these common attributes. Additionally, they can also specify their specific properties.

Start by adding a new authenticated datasource named "Mailjet" with the following details (Figure 5-11):

- URL: Specify the base URL of the API. It should specify the location of Mailjet API (`https://api.mailjet.com`).

- Headers: You can specify multiple headers, which must be passed in the API. Add the content type as the key in the first column and application/json as the value in the next column.

- Authentication type: Specify "Basic" as the type of authentication.

- Authentication: Add the API key as the username and the API secret as the password.

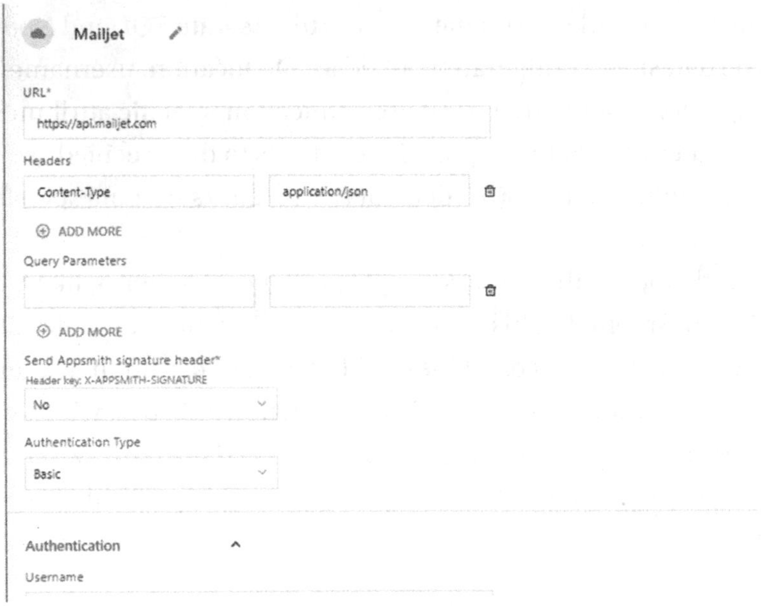

Figure 5-11. *Mailjet authenticated datasource*

Confirm these details by clicking the "Save" button.

Authenticated API Query

Start by adding an API query under the newly added datasource named "Mailjet." You can either click the "Add New API" button under the added datasource (Figure 5-12), or you can add a new blank API and start typing the API URL. Appsmith will show the available API datasources as you type the service location. You can select a datasource, Mailjet, to apply the corresponding configuration.

Figure 5-12. *Authenticated datasource list*

Mailjet provides a POST API with the required body for sending emails. The request body specifies the details, like from, to, subject, message, etc. You must substitute these values from the selected customer details. In previous chapters, you executed a query by invoking the Execute function of the Appsmith Query object. The Execute function supports an option parameter named params. The params argument can be used to pass JSON values at runtime for query executions. In Chapter 4, you performed query executions by passing parameters. You will use the same mechanism here as well and pass values to the REST API on invocation. The params argument will have a JSON value with the selected customer details.

```
{ "Messages":[{
"From": { "Email": "admin@example.com", "Name": "Admin" },
 "To": [ { "Email": {{ this.params.details.rental_customer }},
"Name": {{ this.params.details.first_name }} }],
"Subject": {{ `${this.params.details.rental_inventory}  Movie
Pending Return.`}} ,
"HtmlPart":  {{ `Hi ${this.params.details.first_name}<br>There
is a movie pending in your name. Please contact the nearest
store to return it immediately. <br>regards<br>Admin` }} }]}
```

This code shows how to use the params values to create an appropriate email request body. The details object contains the entire customer details with different attributes for name, email, etc. These attributes are then used in individual request body fields. Now that all details are available, add a new API named email with the following configuration (Figure 5-13):

- Type: POST

- Location: The location of Mailjet Send API (https:// api.mailjet.com/v3.1/send)

- Body: Details of the send request.

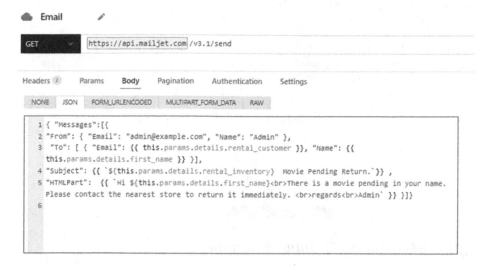

Figure 5-13. *Mailjet Send Mail query*

Plumbing Code

The created `email` query needs to be invoked on customer selection. The application user will select a customer and then confirm the notification request. This confirmation is added using navigation flows and modal dialogs, as discussed in Chapter 4.

The `pending_return_list` table supports customer selection by default. The selected record is available as a selected row attribute of the table. Next, add a "Reminder" button to open a confirmation dialog (Figure 5-14). The dialog can open a modal window to confirm the details before sending the notification.

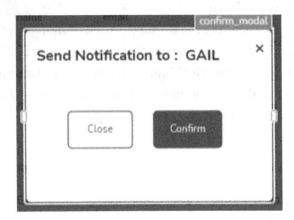

first_name	last_name	email	title	rental_da...
LOUISE	JENKINS	LOUISE.JENKINS@sakilacustomer.org	FRISCO FORREST	14/02/2006
WILLIE	HOWELL	WILLIE.HOWELL@sakilacustomer.org	TITANS JERK	14/02/2006
EMILY	DIAZ	EMILY.DIAZ@sakilacustomer.org	CONNECTION MICROCOSMOS	14/02/2006
LAURIE	LAWRENCE	LAURIE.LAWRENCE@sakilacustomer.org	HAUNTED ANTITRUST	14/02/2006
LISA	ANDERSON	LISA.ANDERSON@sakilacustomer.org	BULL SHAWSHANK	14/02/2006
FREDDIE	DUGGAN	FREDDIE.DUGGAN@sakilacustomer.org	GHOST GROUNDHOG	14/02/2006
HEATHER	MORRIS	HEATHER.MORRIS@sakilacustomer.org	PEACH INNOCENT	14/02/2006
ROLAND	SOUTH	ROLAND.SOUTH@sakilacustomer.org	SUIT WALLS	14/02/2006

Figure 5-14. *Adding "Reminder" button*

Add a modal widget to the application canvas. The modal widget offers "Label," "Confirm," and "Close" buttons. The label can be enabled to print the selected customer name (Figure 5-15). Add the following to the Modal label component:

```
Send Notification to : {{pending_return_list.selectedRow.
first_name}}
```

Figure 5-15. *Confirm customer name*

Update the "Confirm" button configuration to execute the email query with the customer details. Accomplish this by confirming "Execution of Query" as part of the onClick behavior of the button. Additionally, make sure to pass parameters JSON with details attribute as shown here:

```
{{{
  "details": pending_list.selectedRow
}}}
```

In the preceding section, you added the features of customer selection, review, and email notification. The entire process works for a single selected record and must be repeated several times for multiple records. In the next section, you will work with the Appsmith JavaScript object and improve the user experience with multiple rows selection.

Working with JS Objects

In Chapter 4, you worked with the Appsmith JavaScript objects and the different types of supported functions. These functions provide a programmatic way of interacting with different Appsmith components, like widgets and queries. Appsmith's JS framework also offers several functions that can be used to perform varied actions, like conditional navigation, opening and closing interactive elements, creating application state, etc. The JS object provides a powerful construct to create complex logic and an enriched user experience. You can use JS objects to redefine the application user experience, as outlined in the next section.

Hands-on: Customer Multi-selection

The RetroReels Reminder app is able to determine the list of customers with overdue returns and send email notifications. Often an application user needs to send notifications to multiple people. She can only send notifications one at a time, and thus, the entire process consumes much effort. Thus, the application must adopt the following requirements to improve the user experience:

- User should be able to select multiple customers and send all notifications at once.

- User can also provide a specific message for selected customers instead of a generic reminder.

JS Object

These stated requirements need to offer multiple record selections. But then you can't show all customer details on the modal dialog. It would be better to show just two customer names and then truncate with the number of selected customers. Lastly, on confirmations, the authenticated email API, created previously, must be invoked multiple times.

As a first step, toggle the multi-row selection feature on the pending_return_list table. This configuration enables a radio button in front of every row to be selected. Next, update the Modal label to display a truncated text. The text must be generated from a synchronous function, as discussed in Chapter 4. Thus, add a new JS object, named notify, by clicking on the accordion icon (+) against Queries / JS, in the left-hand menu. The object will open a JS editor to specify the associated JS code. As discussed in Chapter 4, the JS object code must conform to a particular structure with export default keywords. Next, add a function to generate truncated customer names.

```
export default {
getCustomernames: () => {
          let totalNames = pending_list.selectedRows.length
          let names = pending_list.selectedRows
              .slice(0,3)
              .map((data, pos) =>{
```

```
            let name = data.first_name
                if (pos==2 ) {
                    name =`and
                    ${totalNames-2} more`
                }
            return name
        })
        .join();
    return names;
    }
}
```

This function is simple JavaScript, where you select the top three records of the array of the selected rows. Then, extract the names of the top two records and replace the third name with the "n more" string (Figure 5-16). You can execute the function by clicking the "RUN" button on the top-right corner. Please make sure to select a few records on the pending_return_list table. The just-added function must be executed at the popup of the Modal dialog. Update the modal label component with the function invocation.

```
Send Notification to : {{notify.getCustomernames()}}
```

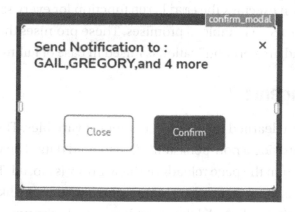

Figure 5-16. *Confirm multiple customer names*

167

As discussed previously, the email query supports only single customer details. Thus, it must be invoked multiple times to send notifications to all selected customers. Appsmith executes all queries asynchronously. The function must wait for the query completion to raise alerts if there are failures. In Chapter 4, you worked with promises to execute asynchronous functions. Promises provide a way to handle callbacks without creating cyclic dependencies in the code. Thus, add another function to execute the email query and raise failure alerts:

```
export default {
    getCustomernames: () => {
        // removed for Brevity
    },
    sendEmail: () => {
        let ack=pending_retrun_list.selectedRows.map(r =>
        email.run({"details": r}));
        Promise.all(ack)
            .catch(() => showAlert("Error in sending mail
                something went wrong"))
    }
}
```

This function executes the email.run function for every selected record and returns an iterable of promises. These promises then wait for completion, and an alert notification is raised in case of failures.

State Management

In Chapter 4, you learned that JS objects support variables. These variables can provide a non-persistent state to hold data. The variables are refreshed when the page reloads or the window is closed. This storage can fit many use cases that require temporary data holding, like payment order confirmation, selected delivery address, etc. In the next section, you will get hands-on with how JS object variables can be used to provide a message override feature. *A user can also provide a specific message for selected customers instead of a generic reminder.*

Variables and functions can't be created outside of the export default { } declaration.

Previously, you integrated with Mailjet notification services via an authenticated API query named email. The email query generated its request body from the supplied arguments. Thus, the query has the logic of generating email message text. The request body editor offers limited controls and can't be configured programmatically. As a first step, move the request body generation to the sendEmail JS function. You can also optimize the implementation by generating all messages and invoking the Email query once instead of invoking the Email query per selected records.

```
sendEmail: () => {
        let msglist=pending_retrun_list.selectedRows.map(r => {
            return { "From": { "Email": "admin@example.
            com", "Name": "Sample" } ,
                    "To": [ { "Email": r.rental_customer,
                    "Name": r.first_name }],
                    "Subject": `${r.rental_inventory}  Movie
                    Pending Return.` ,
        "HTMLPart": `Hi ${r.first_name}<br>There is a movie
        pending in your name. Please contact the nearest store
        to return it immediately. <br>regards<br>Admin`};
            });

    let ack=email.run({"details": msglist});
    Promise.all(ack)
        .catch((e) => {
```

```
        showAlert("Error in sending mail something went
    wrong");
            })
    },
```

This code generates mail details for all selected customers. It then collects these details in an array and invokes the email query. The query passes the array in the request body and sends the request to the Mailjet API.

```
{ "Messages": {{this.params.details}} }
```

Now that the JS object has the logic to generate email text, you can customize it as per the business. But first, please validate if the email sending is working as expected.

Add Variables

As per the provided specification, you need to have a generic message that is used for sending mail. However, an internal user can provide a new specific message for selected customers. This can be accomplished by adding a variable for holding the email message.

```
email : { msg : "Hi ${this.cust_record.first_name} <br>There is
a movie pending in your name. Please contact the nearest store
to return it immediately. <br>regards<br>Admin"},
```

The sendEmail function is updated to generate email configuration based on the preceding variable.

```
sendEmail: () => {
    const generateMsg = () => {
            return "`"+this.email.msg+"`;"
    };

    let msglist=pending_return_list.selectedRows.map(r => {
```

```
        this.cust_record = r;
        return { "From": this.from_address ,
        "To": [ { "Email": r.rental_customer, "Name":
        r.first_name }],
        "Subject": `${r.rental_inventory}  Movie Pending
        Return.` ,
        "HTMLPart": eval?.(generateMsg())};
        });
```

```
// Removed for Brevity
},
```

In this method, the variable is used to hold a JS template literal. This literal is evaluated at runtime by supplying the required arguments to generate the main text.

The code here generated message content by invoking `eval` indirectly. Indirect `eval` and function constructor are not recommended and are shown as linting issues.

Update Variables

In the previous section, you used the JS object variable to generate email message text. The variable can be used to render text in UI components, like a text editor or label. But it can't be updated directly from the UI component. Instead, you must invoke a function and pass the value from the UI component on an action, say, an `onClick` event. The function can then update the variable value, as shown here:

```
updateEmailMsg : (text) => {
     this. email.msg = text
},
```

Add a button named `update_email_msg` to provide the feature of email message updates (Figure 5-17). The `update_email_msg` button needs to open a Modal window, so add a new Modal Window widget to the application. Also, update the `onClick` button action to open the newly added Modal window.

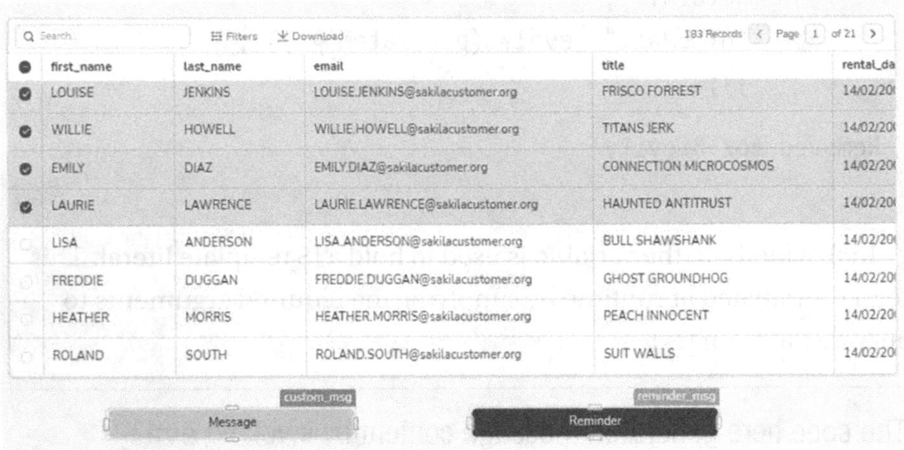

Figure 5-17. *Specific message feature*

The Modal window needs a rich text editor, so add the required widget. The editor must display the text from the JS object variable. Update the default text field to determine the value:

`{{notify.email.msg}}`

The editor now displays the main text (Figure 5-18). A user can update it and click the "Confirm" button. This button executes a close modal action. It also needs to invoke an update function to update the `notify.email.msg` variable.

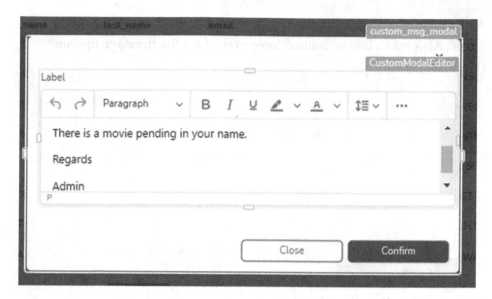

Figure 5-18. *Message Editor window*

This feature allows a user to update email messages before selecting customers. Customers notified after the email message update will receive emails with the updated message. Users can then reload the page and return to the default mail message.

Session State Management

In the previous section, you worked with JS objects for keeping a state. JS objects have a lifetime of the page they are associated with. If you move to a different page, the JS object variables are reset to their initial values. Thus, the objects are not suited for multi-page applications.

In the Reminder app, open a Modal dialog to provide the specific message. Instead of the current approach, add a new page to the Reminder application called Email Settings. The page can be enhanced to provide several mailing features, like a message editor, scheduled delivery, etc.

Adding a message editor to the window is sufficient for our current scope. Also, add a button named Save to confirm the message update (Figure 5-19).

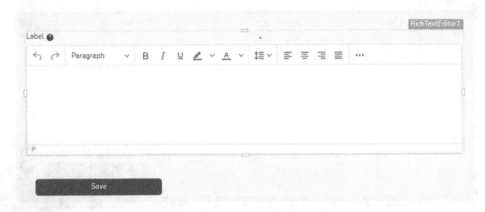

Figure 5-19. *Email setting page*

Next, the application must propagate data across the just created two pages. You can leverage browser local storage using Appsmith-provided store value/remove value/clear store APIs. As discussed in the storage section of Chapter 4, these APIs offer sessions and persistent storage of values. Unlike the session state, which would reset the value on logout/close, the persistence state would keep a value across different users.

The widget actions, like the OnClick event, support only persistent state storage. Thus, add a new JS object named settings. Add a function to save the user-provided message in a key—say, mailmsg.

```
export default {
     saveMailMsg: (txt) => {
           storeValue("mailmsg", txt, false)
     }
}
```

It is important to note that the storeValue method has three arguments: key, value, and storage flag. Invoke the method, with editor text, as part of the onClick behavior of the "Save" button.

The editor does not show the main text saved by the user. Thus, update the default value property of the editor to look up the mailmsg key.

```
{{ appsmith.store.mailmsg }}
```

The Appsmith framework supports key lookup, from the store object, for reading values irrespective of the type of state. The preceding code displays text once saved by the user. Alternatively, you can add a JS function to either read the key or provide a placeholder value.

```
export default {
saveMailMsg: (txt) => {
          storeValue("mailmsg", txt, false)
     },
     readText : () =>{
              appsmith.store.mailmsg? appsmith.store.mailmsg:
              "Placeholder Text"
     }
}
```

Next, you must update the sendEmail function on the Home page to read the mailmsg storage key and use it for message generation.

Embed Appsmith Applications

Web pages have the concept of embedding external content, which means inserting content that is not served by the same server as the web page. You can embed various things, like forms for user signup, maps for location services, etc. Marketing teams often work with embedded feeds from various social media platforms to reach out to more people. Embedding low-code applications enables you to offer features that are not envisioned in your website. These embedded components provide value to the users and can offer an improved user experience while accelerating your time to market.

HTML embedding is quite simple. As a start, you must determine the location of the Appsmith application. You can do this by going to Application Settings ➤ Share & Embed.

The Appsmith community version only allows you to embed public applications. This can be a concern while working on the Appsmith cloud. In such scenarios, you can work with the Enterprise version of Appsmith, which offers embedding of private applications as well. However, if you are working with a self-hosted infrastructure, this concern is often mitigated as access is already controlled. Thus, enable public access and generate the embedded URL for the RetroReels Reminder app (`http://appsmithhost/ app/reminder-app/page1-649958f0c7df13345db79bc5?embed=true`).

An Appsmith application URL contains an optional embed attribute. The attribute is required to remove the header bar containing the sign-in button.

Appsmith also provides a hostname check to disallow anonymous embedding and restrict domains that can work with embedded apps. You can either click the Embed restriction icon on the Application Settings or move to the Admin Settings console from the application dashboard's left-hand menu (Figure 5-20). The restriction can be configured as part of Email Settings under the General section. You must select the "limit embedding" option, remove the asterisk (*) domain, and provide your preferred domain.

Embed Settings

○ Allow embedding everywhere NOT RECOMMENDED ❷

◉ Limit embedding to certain URLs

You can add one or more URLs

'self' ✕   * ✕

○ Disable embedding everywhere

Figure 5-20. *Embedded domain check*

Next, update the HTML code of the web page with an Iframe component referring to the location of the app:

```
<iframe src="http://appsmithhost/app/reminder-app/page1-649958f
0c7df13345db79bc5?embed=true" />
```

The current application does not require any special permissions. In scenarios where the Appsmith application requires special permission, like camera, microphone, geolocation, etc., you would need an additional `allow` attribute to delegate these permissions.

Summary

The chapter provides a foundation for working with APIs in the Appsmith framework. GraphQL APIs are very good at serving data with user-specified fields. However, REST APIs are good at handling anything like data fetch, executing actions, etc. Appsmith integration with both of them is very minimalistic. Both are available in two variants: authenticated and non-authenticated versions. They offer the inheritance of headers, authentication, etc. APIs can be used with JS objects to provide an enriched user experience. The chapter also discussed the various ways of state propagation, like query parameters, JS object variables, and application-wide storage. The next chapter provides the foundation for application authentication and access control.

CHAPTER 6

Access Control

Application security is essential to safeguard your data and business processes. The practice consists of several techniques, like authentication, authorization, vulnerability scanning, etc. Authentication is the process of confirming that a user is who they say they are. Typically, this can be accomplished by requiring the user to provide a username and password. Post authentication, the application must authorize if the user has the permissions needed for access. Authorization can also be based on the domain logic. The application needs to perform the preceding checks before serving every user action. Asking the user to submit this information every time leads to a poor user experience. Thus, the application authentication flow validates the user credentials and supports means of fetching the information again. Traditional applications used to offer this by saving the user details in the session associated with the user login. Modern applications do not store this information and instead encrypt the information in a JSON web token passed with each request.

Application identity management and authentication is an aspirational feature of Low Code Development Platforms (LCDPs). Appsmith does not offer application authentication out of the box. Alternatively, you can integrate several third-party platforms, like Google Firebase, Supabase, and AWS Amplify, that provide authentication in several ways, like username–password or social login using Google, Facebook, etc. In this chapter, you will work with Appsmith integration with Google Firebase. However, Appsmith offers user management to control who has permission to create and update applications on the platform or perform server updates.

© Rahul Sharma and Rajat Arora 2023
R. Sharma and R. Arora, *Low-Code Development with Appsmith*,
https://doi.org/10.1007/978-1-4842-9813-8_6

Application Authentication

Password authentication is the most basic form of authentication. Users can be asked to create a username and a password on a signup form. Alternatively, internal users can be provided with their credentials via a separate onboarding process. It is essential to note that the entire signup process consists of several steps, like validating username uniqueness, enforcing password rules, and then saving them in an encrypted manner. After this, a user must pass these credentials in every request. All these requirements must be developed as server-side application programming interface (API) features.

Appsmith does not provide an out-of-the-box user authentication feature for applications. You can build this feature using a database query, as in Chapter 4. However, it is not recommended to do this as there are several issues, like keeping unencrypted passwords, unmasked Personally Identifiable Information (PII) user data, and unsupported features like social auth and multi-factor auth. Also, the overall effort can quickly expand to offer signup-associated flows, like email verification, password reset, etc. Instead, you can integrate a third-party authentication platform, as discussed next.

Set Up Firebase

Google Firebase is an application development platform that offers a suite of server-side components, like database, authentication, push notifications, and cloud hosting, for quickly developing mobile and web applications. All these functions are provided as pluggable, ready-made features with SDKs in several development languages like JS, Python, Kotlin, etc. Moreover, Firebase lets you bootstrap your application with several add-on Google services like ads and analytics.

Applications that require establishing the identity of the user can accomplish this with the authentication feature of Firebase. Firebase supports authentication using passwords, emails, phone numbers, highly known identity providers like Google, Facebook and Twitter, and many more. It offers almost all sign-in features, like sign up, log in, social sign-in methods, forget password reset/change, multi-factor verification, etc. Firebase is a versatile product outside the scope of this book. This section will discuss details that are necessary for the integration of Firebase authentication. Please look into Firebase documentation to know more about its offerings.

Firebase is a cloud platform, so sign up for platform access using your email. Next, you must add a project with a unique name in the Firebase console. The project page (shown in Figure 6-1) will also list your existing Google Cloud applications, if any. You can select them to associate Firebase services with the respective application.

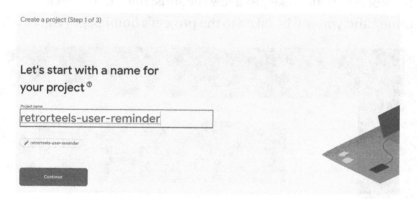

Figure 6-1. *Firebase project*

The next step is optional—to set up Google Analytics for the project (Figure 6-2). For now, toggle the Google Analytics setup as it is not required in RetroReels. Finally, accept the terms and click "Create project."

Figure 6-2. *Google Analytics*

The process should take just a few seconds; once done, click "Continue," and you will be taken to the project's homepage (Figure 6-3).

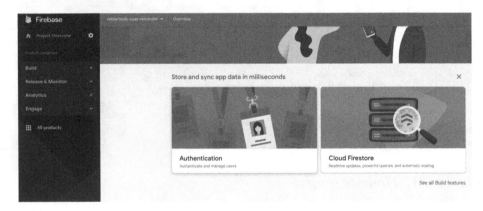

Figure 6-3. *Firebase project console*

Enable Authentication

As discussed previously, Firebase provides a suite of services, of which authentication is one (Figure 6-4). Before using the email/password sign-in method in the Appsmith RetroReels application, you must enable the sign-in method in the Firebase console by following the steps outlined here:

- Head to our Firebase project dashboard. Click the dropdown menu on the sidebar to show all products.

- Click the "Build" option, and then click the "Authentication" option to open the Auth section, and then click "Get started."

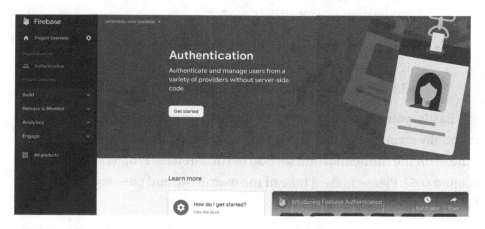

Figure 6-4. *Firebase Authentication console*

- Next, you need to configure the login method. Click on "Setup sign-in method" and select "Email/Password" from the list (Figure 6-5) of Native providers.

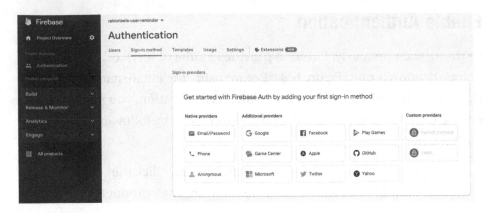

Figure 6-5. *Sign-in auth providers*

- Click the toggle button to enable email/password authentication and click "Save."

- Optionally, you can also offer the email/password signup option to let users sign up using their email address and password and click "Save."

Lastly, you must add a few users that can be authenticated. Thus, manually create password-authenticated users by clicking the "Add User" button on the Authentication section of the Firebase Project Console (Figure 6-6). Please make a note of the username and password, as this will be required later in the chapter.

Figure 6-6. *Add user*

Firebase API

Firebase provides REST APIs for all services, including authentication. These APIs allow you to perform authentication and user management functions, such as creating new users, signing in, or editing or deleting existing users. The REST API must be invoked with a Firebase API key. It is a secret token that is generated when you add services to a Firebase project. If an API key is compromised, unauthorized users can gain access to our Firebase project and its data. Since Firebase projects can store sensitive user data such as passwords and personal details, keeping the API key confidential is imperative.

- Open the project's settings (Figure 6-7) by clicking the gear at the top of the left-side panel.

Figure 6-7. *Firebase project settings*

- The key can be found listed under the Your Project section

Configure Authentication

In the previous section, you configured Firebase for authentication and added a few users. Next, you must integrate Firebase authentication with Appsmith applications via the REST API. Appsmith REST API integration was discussed in detail in Chapter 5. This section covers the nuances specific to authentication over REST API.

Hands-on

Previously, Chapter 5 provided hands-on experience by working on a reminder use case of RetroReels. The Reminder application allowed users to identify customers with pending returns. These customers can be nudged by email notifications sent from the Reminder application.

The current Reminder application is not secured; anyone can access it to send out notifications. There are several risks, like anonymous usage and customer abuse, associated with this approach. Thus, RetroReels wants to deploy access control to limit the app to an authorized set of users.

Login Page

Under the proposed flow, a User Login page will be the Reminder application's entry point. The user can only access the Reminder dashboard after providing the correct credentials. An error message will be displayed on the screen in case of credentials mismatch.

Select the Reminder app for edit from the Appsmith applications dashboard. Add a new page named "Login." This page should be the application's landing page; thus, toggle the "Set as Homepage" configuration from page settings.

Add a Container widget named loginContainer that can be used to control the size, position, and styles of components used in the Login page. You can use a JSON form, covered in Chapter 4, to generate the login details form (Figure 6-8). Update the form title to Login and the JSON snippet in the Source Data field to this:

```
{
        "username": "",
        "password": ""
}
```

Figure 6-8. *Login page*

The form fields are displayed in lexicographic order, so rearrange them using the right-hand sidebar Field Configuration section. The default input type of each JSON form field is Text. Thus, using the Field Configuration section, you must change the Password field from Text input to Password Input.

Now, the application has two pages, viz login, and home pages. Appsmith, by default, adds a navigation bar as part of the application header. The navigation bar will show both pages, and the user can click and move between the two pages without any check. This must not be allowed; the authentication flow should show the required page. Thus, turn off the navigation bar feature from the Application settings.

Login Query

The Login page must capture the username and password and validate it using Firebase REST APIs for authentication. These APIs must be invoked with an API key, a secret token associated with the Firebase account. This secret must not be stored in plaintext. Start by creating an authenticated API data source named Firebase (Figure 6-9), which can keep the API key encrypted.

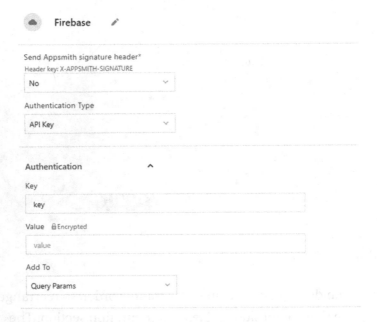

Figure 6-9. *Firebase datasource*

The datasource should have the following configuration:

- URL set to `https://identitytoolkit.googleapis.com`

- API key as the authentication type option

- Under the authentication section, specify the "Add to" option as Query Params.

- Specify the request parameter as Key and the corresponding API token.

Next, add an authenticated API, named auth, under the Firebase data source (Figure 6-10). Authenticated API was covered in Chapter 5. Add a new API with the following configuration:

- Request Type as Post

- URL set to [Firebase URL]/v1/
  accounts:signInWithPassword

- Specify the username and password under the body as JSON. This is accomplished by binding JSONForm1 fields of the Login page.

```
{{ {
        "email": JSONForm1.formData.usernamae,
        "password":JSONForm1.formData.password
}}}
```

Figure 6-10. *Firebase sign-in API*

189

You should be able to validate the API by providing the credentials of the manually added Firebase user in the form and clicking the "RUN query" button on the authenticated API console. The query response will have a JSON structure with user details like email, token, kind, etc.

```
{
  "kind": "identitytoolkit#VerifyPasswordResponse",
  "localId": "K2jH2G3jjiZuBThpxJKbHD8687B3",
  "email": "user1@retroreels.com",
  "idToken": "eyJhbGciOiJSUzI1NiIsImtpZCI.............."
// Truncated for Brevity
}
```

Plumbing

Before moving ahead, let's understand the Firebase authentication response. Besides providing the basic user details, the response contains an identity token specified as the idToken attribute. This identity token is in the JSON Web Token (JWT) format, which can be used to validate the user for other server-side invocations by using the authentication HTTP header parameter. JWT is an open standard defining a compact and self-contained way to transmit information between parties as a JSON object securely. The token is a JSON-encoded representation of a claim or claims transferred between the server and clients. The token contains details related to issue time and expiry time, after which it must be discarded, and a new token must be issued. The token is a URL-safe string that can contain an unlimited amount of data. When a server receives a JWT, it can trust its data, as the source cryptographically signs the JWT. JWT guards against information tampering as it can't be modified.

After executing the query successfully, the application must extract and save the token. You can also extract and save other details, like username and email. The application must also navigate to the Home page. To accomplish the this, you can write a simple JS script as part of the submit onClick event.

```
{{
    Auth.run(() => {
        const jwt = Auth?.data?.idToken;
        // -15 as the length if string ".retroreels.com"
        const uname = Auth?.data?.email.slice(0, -15);
        if (jwt) {
            storeValue('jwt', jwt);
            storeValue('uname', uname);
            navigateTo('Home', {});
        } else {
            showAlert('Login failed!', 'error');
        }
    })
}}
```

There are several changes required on the existing Home page as well (Figure 6-11). First, add a container named pageContainer, and then move all page components like table and buttons inside it. Programmatically update the visibility of the container to show only when the Appsmith store has a valid JWT.

```
{{appsmith?.store?.jwt !== undefined }}
```

Figure 6-11. *Dashboard*

Next, you must add a header with a "Logout" button. Additionally, the header can also display the username and any other details. The logout action must clear the Appsmith store to discard the user identity and move to the Login page. You can perform the same by executing the following JS as part of Logout onClick.

```
{{
  (() => {
    clearStore()
    navigateTo("Login");
  })()
}}
```

In this section, you used Firebase to add authentication. It can be extended to provide authorization based on Firestore and blocking functions. The entire process is well beyond the scope of the book and requires good knowledge of JS or Python.

Appsmith Platform Authentication

The preceding section outlined the process of authentication for applications developed in Appsmith. Appsmith is a web application that several users can leverage. So far, you have been using the Appsmith open-source edition as the server admin. Appsmith allows the onboarding of users in several ways, like email signup, Google authentication, or SAML authentication (for organization SSO). For enterprise needs, Appsmith offers seamless integration with various popular SAML providers, like Active Directory and Auth0. SAML integration would need knowledge of enterprise-level identity management tools and is well beyond the scope of the book.

Previously, you used email-based signup to create an admin user. The email-based signup can be used to sign up more users. Alternatively, authentication with Google is quite simple and can be handy if your organization works with Google Workspace accounts. You must sign up for Google Cloud and create a project; e.g., retroreels-reminders-auth. You would need to complete the "configuring the user consent display" process before you can generate an OAuth client ID and secret. The OAuth consent screen informs the users of the details of your app and what kind of data they are allowing your app to access. Once done, you can generate an OAuth client ID and secret by providing the correct JavaScript origin URL and redirect URL details. These details are available under Google Authentication in the Appsmith settings console.

Once you have the OAuth client ID and secret details, add the Client ID, client secret, and allowed domains to Google Authentication in the Appsmith settings console (Figure 6-12). Save the configuration and restart the server.

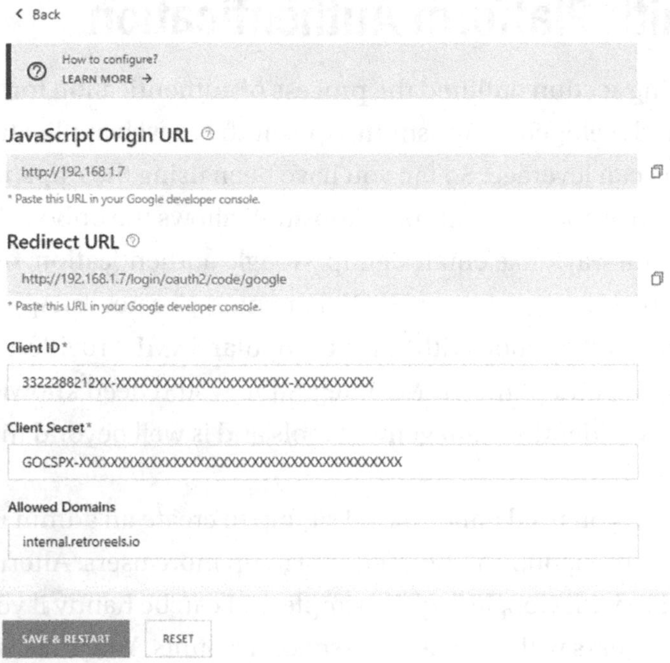

< Back

? How to configure?
  LEARN MORE →

JavaScript Origin URL ⓘ

http://192.168.1.7

* Paste this URL in your Google developer console.

Redirect URL ⓘ

http://192.168.1.7/login/oauth2/code/google

* Paste this URL in your Google developer console.

Client ID *

3322288212XX-XXXXXXXXXXXXXXXXXXXXXXX-XXXXXXXXXX

Client Secret *

GOCSPX-XXXXXXXXXXXXXXXXXXXXXXXXXXXXXXXXXXXXXXXXXX

Allowed Domains

internal.retroreels.io

SAVE & RESTART   RESET

Figure 6-12. *Google OAuth sign-in*

Appsmith Roles

Every user in Appsmith is associated with a role, and each role has a set
of permissions. These permissions determine the actions that a user can
perform. The open-source version comes bundled with the roles detailed
in Table 6-1.

Table 6-1. *Appsmith Roles*

	Administrator	Developer	Viewer
Appsmith Server Management	Y	N	N
Workspace Management (Create/ Delete)	Y	Y	N
Application Management (Create/Update/ Delete)	Y	Y	N
Application Templates	Y	Y	N
View Applications	Y	Y	Y
Invite Users	Y	Y	Y

It is important to note that even though many actions are available in Appsmith, there are only three roles in the open-source edition. These roles are only required for teams that are developing or testing applications in Appsmith. These users can develop, test, and validate the application. Once the application has been deployed with public access, it can be accessed by users who do not require Appsmith login.

Appsmith business edition offers granular permissions, which can be clubbed to form custom roles. These custom roles can be used across several teams beyond active development, like marketing, app sec, etc. In addition to this, the business edition also offers audit logs. These logs can track changes to workspaces, apps, pages, data sources, queries, and JS objects via a central console.

Summary

The chapter discussed the most common use case of application authentication. Appsmith currently lacks support for authentication, but it can be extended with several third-party platforms like Google Firebase to. Besides authentication, these third-party backend platforms provide a suite of servers that Appsmith developers can leverage. While applications developed with Appsmith need external integrations, the platform offers several ways to onboard developers, testers, business analysts, etc., to the Appsmith platform. The open-source edition came bundled with signup forms and can be extended with Google Workspace integration. Each of these users must be associated with built-in roles that define the permissions provided to the platform user. Sometimes, applications fail to perform as expected and may not report any errors. In such a scenario, finding and resolving the issue can be challenging. The next chapter will discuss ways of debugging and troubleshooting Appsmith applications.

CHAPTER 7

Error Handling and Troubleshooting

In the world of application development, errors and issues are inevitable, even when using low-code development tools like Appsmith. Whether it's a bug in the code, a malfunctioning database query, or a JavaScript error, understanding how to effectively handle and troubleshoot problems is crucial for maintaining the stability and functionality of your applications.

In this chapter, we will equip you with the knowledge and tools needed to identify, diagnose, and resolve errors in your Appsmith applications. Through this chapter, you will gain a comprehensive understanding of various debugging techniques and strategies, enabling you to tackle a wide range of issues that may arise.

We'll start by exploring the different ways you can debug an Appsmith application. You will learn how to leverage the built-in debugging tools provided by Appsmith and the developer tools available in popular web browsers. These tools will allow you to analyze network requests, inspect console logs, and navigate the widget tree to pinpoint potential issues.

Next, we'll delve into the realm of errors that can occur in your applications. This includes application errors, database errors, and JavaScript errors. You will learn how to interpret error messages and stack traces, helping you identify the root cause of these errors. We'll cover common User Interface (UI)-related issues, data-handling problems, database connection verification, query error diagnosis, and JavaScript debugging techniques.

© Rahul Sharma and Rajat Arora 2023
R. Sharma and R. Arora, *Low-Code Development with Appsmith*,
https://doi.org/10.1007/978-1-4842-9813-8_7

Throughout the chapter, we will share practical examples, real-world scenarios, and best practices to reinforce your understanding of error handling and troubleshooting. Additionally, we'll discuss additional tips for effective logging, error tracking, version control, and collaboration with the Appsmith community and support.

By the end of this chapter, you will possess the skills and knowledge required to confidently tackle errors and troubleshoot issues in your Appsmith applications. So, let's dive in and embark on this journey of mastering error handling and troubleshooting in Appsmith!

A Framework for Effective Bug Investigation

When encountering unexpected behavior or errors in software development, the troubleshooting process becomes vital in identifying and resolving issues efficiently. This section provides an overview of the troubleshooting process, offering a basic framework to guide you in your bug investigation endeavors. While specific debugging techniques and tools will be discussed in subsequent sections, understanding the overarching steps of troubleshooting is crucial.

The troubleshooting process typically involves the following key steps:

1. **Reproduce the Issue**: The first step is to reproduce the issue consistently. By recreating the problem, you gain a clear understanding of the error's scope and conditions. In web development, this might involve replicating a malfunctioning website feature by following a specific sequence of user interactions. Similarly, in Appsmith app development, you might need to identify the specific inputs or actions that trigger the unexpected behavior.

2. **Understand the Expected Behavior:** To effectively troubleshoot, it's crucial to have a clear understanding of the expected behavior of the application or feature in question. This can be achieved by referring to the project requirements, design documentation, or user stories. By contrasting the expected behavior against the observed behavior, you can pinpoint the potential source of the issue.

   For example, in web development, if a form submission fails to save data to the database, understanding the expected behavior would involve knowing which fields should be captured and how the data should be persisted.

3. **Isolate the Issue:** Once you have established the expected behavior and reproduced the issue, the next step is to isolate the problem. This entails identifying the specific component, module, or section of code that is responsible for the unexpected behavior. Isolating the issue helps narrow down your focus and reduces the scope of investigation.

   In Appsmith, isolating the issue could mean identifying the specific widget, API, or database query that is causing the error.

4. **Gather Information:** Gathering relevant information about the issue is crucial for effective troubleshooting. This includes examining error messages, reviewing logs, and analyzing the state of the application at the time of the error. By collecting pertinent information, you gain valuable insights that can help in identifying the root cause of the problem.

In Appsmith, you can gather information by examining the error messages displayed in the console, inspecting the widget tree, and reviewing the query pane for database-related issues.

5. **Formulate Hypotheses**: Based on the information gathered, you can formulate hypotheses about the potential causes of the issue. These hypotheses serve as starting points for further investigation. Consider all possible factors, such as code errors, incorrect configurations, or external dependencies.

6. **Test and Validate**: Once you have formulated hypotheses, it's essential to test and validate them systematically. This involves performing targeted tests, modifying code or configurations as needed, and observing the impact of each change. Through experimentation and validation, you gain insights into the validity of your hypotheses and move closer to resolving the issue.

   In Appsmith, you can test hypotheses by modifying widget configurations, adjusting API calls, or inspecting query results.

Remember, the troubleshooting process is iterative, and it may require multiple cycles of investigation, testing, and validation to identify and resolve the issue effectively. By following these fundamental steps and utilizing the debugging techniques and tools discussed in the subsequent sections, you'll be equipped to navigate the complexities of bug investigation in both web development and Appsmith app development.

Having established a framework for effective bug investigation, it's time to explore a powerful tool that can greatly assist in the debugging process: the console object. The console object is a valuable resource provided by Appsmith, offering developers the ability to log messages and gain valuable insights during the debugging process. By leveraging the console object, you can enhance your ability to identify and resolve errors in your Appsmith applications. Let's dive into the details of the console object and discover how it can elevate your debugging capabilities.

The Console Object

In the world of application development, effective debugging is vital for identifying and resolving errors. Appsmith provides developers with a powerful tool called the console object. The console object empowers developers to log messages and gain valuable insights during the debugging process.

With the console object, developers can output information, track code flow, and diagnose issues efficiently. It offers various methods for logging, including standard logs, warnings, and errors. By leveraging the console object, developers can enhance the quality and performance of their Appsmith applications.

The console object provides an interface to the web browser's console (not to be confused with the JavaScript console object). It's akin to a developer's diary, where every significant event or action that occurs in your app can be logged. It provides valuable information about the state and behavior of your application in real time, enabling you to understand the flow of data, catch errors, and debug with greater ease.

The Appsmith console object comes packed with a variety of methods, each designed to cater to a specific logging need:

1. **`console.log(message: any)`**: This is the most basic type of logging. These logs can be used during development to provide detailed insights into the internal workings of your application. They help trace the flow of the code, monitor variable values,

201

and identify specific areas of interest. Such log statements are generally short lived, and can be safely removed from the code after development finishes. For example:

- `"Entering loop iteration {i} in {function}"`

- `"Value of variable 'data' at {location}: {value}"`

2. **console.info(message: any)**: This is generally used to display informational messages that are less critical. It can be helpful in understanding the paths your code is taking, and also provide context and details about the execution flow of your application. They can help track significant events or milestones during runtime. For example:

- `"User registration initiated: {username}"`

- `"API request sent to retrieve data for user {id}"`

3. **console.warn(message: any)**: As the name suggests, this method is used to log warning messages that alert you about potential issues that might not be errors but still deserve attention. They serve as proactive indicators of potential problems. For example:

- `"Invalid input detected in form field: {field}"`

- `"Deprecated function 'calculateTotal()' uses in {component}"`

4. **console.error(message: any)**: Error logs capture unexpected or exceptional conditions that could disrupt the normal functioning of your application. They help pinpoint issues that need to be addressed and potentially lead to failure. For example:

- "Database connection failed: {error}"

- "Unhandled exception occurred in {function}: {error}"

Here is an example of how to use these methods:

```
console.log("This is a log message.");
console.info("This is an info message.");
console.warn("This is a warning message.");
console.error("This is an error message.");
```

The output of these statements will be displayed in the browser console, each one tagged with its log level (log, info, warn, error). The different log levels not only help in categorizing and filtering your logs, but also assist in visual differentiation as many browsers use different colors and icons for logs of different levels.

To view the logs, you simply need to open your browser's developer tools (usually by pressing F12 [or Ctrl + Shift + I] on your keyboard or right-clicking on your web page and selecting "Inspect") and navigate to the "Console" tab.

By incorporating these different types of log messages, you can effectively track the execution flow, detect potential issues, and gain a deeper understanding of your Appsmith applications. Crafting well-structured log messages with relevant details can greatly enhance your debugging process and contribute to the overall stability and performance of your application.

Logging in RetroReels   Now that you know about different types of logs, identify the different types of log messages that can be included in the RetroReels app.

Using the Browser's Debugger

To enhance our debugging capabilities further, let's explore the browser's built-in debugger. The browser's debugger is a powerful tool that provides a comprehensive set of features to assist in identifying and resolving issues in your Appsmith applications. In this section, we will walk you through the process of using the browser's debugger effectively for JavaScript debugging, step-by-step.

To begin using the browser's debugger, you need to open the browser's Developer Tools. The method for accessing Developer Tools differs depending on the browser you are using. Generally, you can right-click on a web page, select "Inspect" or "Inspect Element," and navigate to the "Console" or "Sources" tab. Alternatively, you can use browser-specific keyboard shortcuts (typically F12 or Ctrl + Shift + I) or access developer tools through the browser's menu.

In the debugger window (Figure 7-1), you will find a top toolbar with buttons for controlling code execution, including stepping into, stepping over, and stepping out of functions. The left-hand panel displays your JavaScript files, allowing you to navigate and select the specific file you want to debug. You can expand the file tree to explore different functions and code blocks within the selected file.

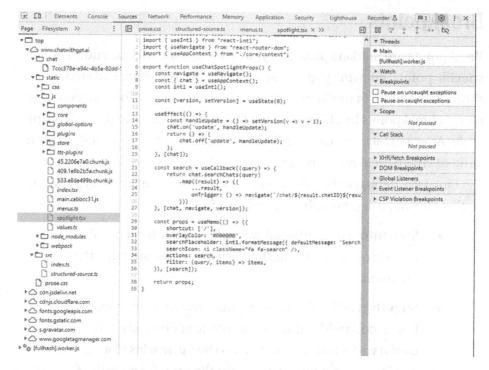

Figure 7-1. *The browser's debugger window*

The right-hand panel of the debugger window provides detailed insights into the execution of your JavaScript code. It includes sections for call stack, breakpoints, scope variables, and watch expressions. The call stack shows the sequence of function calls, helping you understand the flow of your code. Breakpoints can be set by clicking on line numbers in your code, allowing you to pause the execution at specific points to examine the program's state. The scope variables section displays the variables within the current scope, enabling you to inspect their values. Additionally, you can add watch expressions to monitor specific variables or expressions of interest.

Breakpoints

Breakpoints are markers placed in your code to pause its execution at specific points, allowing you to inspect the program's state and step through the code. In the "Sources" tab of the Developer Tools screen, you can set breakpoints by clicking on the line numbers next to the JavaScript code. Alternatively, you can use the "debugger" statement directly in your code to create breakpoints programmatically.

Once the debugger is active and breakpoints are set, you have several options for stepping through your code, as follows:

- **Step Into:** This option allows you to move from one line of code to the next, entering function calls and stepping into them.

- **Step Over:** With this option, you advance to the next line of code without stepping into function calls. It is useful when you want to bypass the intricacies of a particular function and focus on the broader code flow.

- **Step Out:** If you are within a function, this option allows you to step out of the current function and return to its caller. It is helpful when you have stepped into a function and want to return to the higher-level code.

While in a debugging session, you can inspect the values of variables and expressions. In the Developer Tools screen, you will find a "Watch" panel that displays the current values of variables. You can add variables or expressions of interest to this panel, allowing you to monitor their values as you step through the code. This feature provides invaluable insights into the state of your program and helps identify any unexpected or incorrect values.

Using Console and Debugger Together

The browser's console and debugger complement each other in the debugging process. You can log messages to the console using the console object, as we explored earlier. Additionally, when the debugger is active, you can also log messages to the console directly from your code using the `console.log` method. This allows you to monitor specific variables, track the flow of your program, and gain real-time insights while stepping through the code in the debugger.

Types of Errors in AppSmith

As you navigate the development journey of your Appsmith applications, it's important to familiarize yourself with the various types of errors you may encounter. Understanding these error types and their implications will empower you to effectively troubleshoot and resolve issues that may arise during the development and deployment process.

In this section, we will provide a brief introduction to the different types of errors commonly encountered in Appsmith applications. Each error type represents a distinct area or aspect of your application that may require attention. While subsequent sections will delve into some of these error types in detail, this introduction will give you an overview and set the stage for deeper exploration. See the following:

1. **Datasource Errors**: Datasource errors typically occur when there are issues with connecting to or retrieving data from external databases or services. Examples include connection failures, incorrect credentials, or issues with data retrieval.

2. **REST API Errors**: REST API errors can occur when there are problems with communication between your application and external APIs. This can manifest as failed requests, incorrect response formats, authentication issues, or server-side errors returned by the API.

3. **JS Errors**: JavaScript (JS) errors pertain to issues within the client-side JavaScript code of your application. These errors can arise from syntax errors, logical mistakes, undefined variables, or incorrect function usage, resulting in unexpected behavior or application failures.

4. **Deployment Errors**: Deployment errors encompass issues that arise during the process of deploying your Appsmith application to different environments. These can include misconfiguration of deployment settings, dependency mismatches, or issues with deployment platforms.

5. **Application Errors**: Application errors are problems specific to your Appsmith application's implementation and logic. These errors can be caused by incorrect widget configurations, improper event handling, or inconsistent data flow within your application.

6. **Query Errors**: Query errors usually relate to issues within database queries executed by your application. These can include syntax errors, incorrect query logic, or mismatches between query parameters and database schemas.

7. **Widget Errors**: Widget errors pertain to issues related to individual widgets within your Appsmith application. These errors can arise from misconfigured properties, incorrect widget interactions, or conflicts between widget behaviors.

In the subsequent sections, we will delve into some of these error types in detail, exploring their causes, diagnostic approaches, and resolution strategies. By gaining a deeper understanding of these error types, you will be well equipped to tackle specific issues that may arise during your Appsmith application development journey.

So, let's proceed to explore each error type comprehensively and arm ourselves with the knowledge and techniques necessary to handle them effectively in your Appsmith applications.

Datasource Errors

When working with Appsmith, you may encounter various types of datasource errors that can impact the connectivity and retrieval of data from external databases or services. Understanding these error types and their implications will enable you to diagnose and resolve datasource-related issues effectively. Let's explore some common datasource errors you may encounter while building an Appsmith application.

Incorrect Endpoints

Providing incorrect endpoints can lead to errors when establishing a connection or making API calls. This can happen if a typo is present in the URL or if the endpoint has been changed. For instance, specifying an outdated API endpoint or using the wrong port number in a database connection string can result in a "Connection Error" or a "404 – Not Found" error.

Connection Failures / Timeouts

Connection failures can occur when there are issues establishing a
connection with the datasource. This can be due to factors such as incorrect
network configuration, firewall restrictions, or infrastructure-related
problems. For example, if your database server is down, it will result in your
queries getting timed out (Figures 7-2 and 7-3).

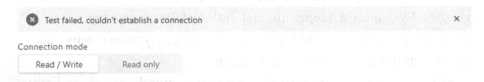

Figure 7-2. *Incorrect endpoint while setting up a new datasource*

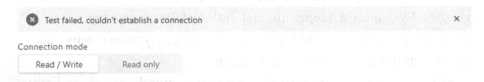

Figure 7-3. *DB connection timed out*

Note that a "Timed Out" error does not necessarily mean that your
database server is not responding. It could be a genuine case of your query
getting timed out. You can investigate further by executing a lightweight
query against your datasource. If that query also times out, chances are
high that it is a problem with the DB server.

Otherwise, you might have to optimize your heavyweight query—or
increase its timeout value (Left Sidebar ➤ Your Query ➤ Settings ➤ Query
Timeout).

Incorrect Credentials

Providing incorrect credentials, such as usernames or passwords, can lead to authentication failures. This can prevent successful access to the datasource. For instance, using an incorrect database username or password can result in an "Access Denied" error. You will encounter this error when creating a new query against a data source whose credentials have changed recently (Figure 7-4).

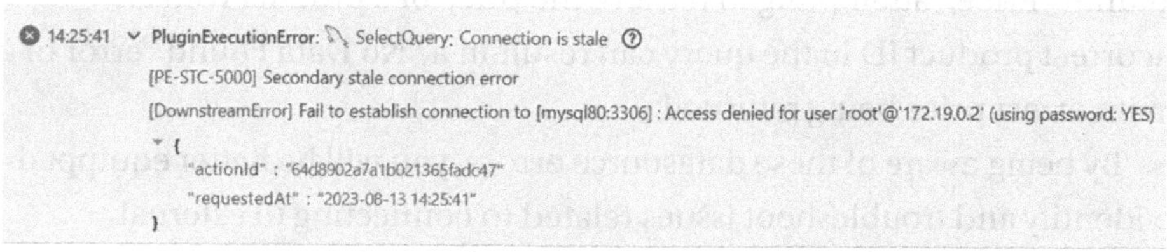

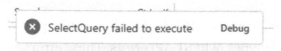

Figure 7-4. "Access Denied" error

In case you have already bound a query to a widget, and the DB credentials change later on, Appsmith will display an alert, as seen in Figure 7-5.

❌ SelectQuery failed to execute   Debug

Figure 7-5. Query failed to execute

When you click on "Debug," you will be shown the same "Access Denied" error just outlined.

To fix this error, you will have to edit your existing datasource and supply it with correct credentials. This can be done by selecting the relevant DB from the datasources section of the left-hand sidebar, clicking on "Edit," and then providing the correct credentials in the Authentication section of the resulting screen.

Issues with Data Retrieval

Problems can arise when fetching data from a datasource. This can include issues such as incomplete or inconsistent data, missing data, or errors in the query logic. For instance, a query to retrieve a specific record from a database may return an empty result set if the data does not exist or if the query conditions are incorrect.

Example: If you have a database table named "Products" with a column "Price," attempting to retrieve the price of a product with an incorrect product ID in the query can result in a "No Data Found" error or an incorrect price being returned.

By being aware of these datasource errors, you will be better equipped to identify and troubleshoot issues related to connecting to external databases or services, retrieving data, and handling authentication. In the subsequent sections, we will explore diagnostic approaches and resolution strategies to effectively address these datasource errors in your Appsmith applications.

REST API Errors

When working with external APIs in your Appsmith applications, you may encounter various types of REST API errors. These errors are defined by the HTTP Error Code mechanism, which provides standardized status codes to indicate the outcome of API requests. Understanding these error codes and their implications will help you effectively handle REST API errors during application development. Let's explore the common REST API errors you may encounter while building an Appsmith application.

Client-Side Errors (4xx)

4xx errors indicate issues on the client side, typically involving problems with the request itself. It's important to understand the following common client-side errors.

404 (Not Found)

This error occurs when the requested resource or API endpoint is not found. It indicates that the URL or endpoint specified in the request is incorrect or does not exist.

400 (Bad Request)

A 400 error signifies that the server cannot process the request due to invalid syntax or missing required parameters. It indicates an issue with the request itself, and hence, it should not be retried as-is. The response may or may not contain a description of what is wrong with the request, so the diagnosis will depend on your reading of the requisite API documentation to figure out the correct request structure.

401 (Unauthorized)

A 401 error indicates that the request requires authentication, and the client has not provided valid credentials or has not authenticated yet.

403 (Forbidden)

A 403 error occurs when the client is authenticated but lacks sufficient permissions to access the requested resource. For example, you may be attempting to update a resource, while using read-only credentials to do so. The request can be retried when proper credentials are obtained.

Server-Side Errors (5xx)

5xx errors signify issues on the server side, indicating a failure in fulfilling the request. It's important to be familiar with the following server-side errors.

500 (Internal Server Error)

A 500 error indicates an unexpected condition on the server that prevented it from fulfilling the request. It can occur due to issues such as code bugs or unhandled exceptions. You may want to notify the maintainer of the API to fix the error before retrying the request.

503 (Service Unavailable)

A 503 error occurs when the server is temporarily unable to handle the request, often due to maintenance, high load, or other transient issues. 503 errors typically resolve themselves once the infrastructural issues are fixed (or when the load on the service lessens).

These are the most common REST API errors that you might encounter while building your applications. However, there are several other error codes that are not discussed here. To know more, you can do the following:

- Read Mozilla Developer Network's documentation on HTTP Response Codes at `https://developer.mozilla.org/en-US/docs/Web/HTTP/Status`.

- Read "HTTP codes as Valentine's Day comics" for a more tongue-in-cheek visualization of the common ones at `https://medium.com/@hanilim/http-codes-as-valentines-day-comics-8c03c805faa0`.

Understanding these REST API errors, whether they are client-side (4xx) or server-side (5xx), will assist you in diagnosing and resolving issues encountered while interacting with external APIs. In the subsequent sections, we will explore diagnostic approaches, error-handling strategies, and best practices to effectively address REST API errors in your Appsmith applications.

JavaScript Errors

During the development of your Appsmith applications, you may encounter various types of JavaScript errors. Understanding these errors and having strategies to debug them effectively will help you identify and resolve issues in your code. Let's explore some common JavaScript errors you may encounter while building an Appsmith application.

Syntax Errors

Syntax errors occur when there are mistakes in the structure or formatting of your JavaScript code. These errors prevent the code from being executed and are typically identified during the parsing phase. Example:

```
if (condition {
    // Missing closing parenthesis
    // Syntax Error: Unexpected token '{'
}
```

To debug such errors, carefully review your code and identify the line where the error occurs. Check for missing parentheses, semicolons, or mismatched brackets. Moreover, Appsmith's JavaScript editor will be your powerful ally in identifying and correcting these errors, as it highlights errors and warnings in your code as you type.

Reference Errors

Reference errors occur when you try to access a variable or function that is not defined or is out of scope. Example:

```
console.log(myVariable); // ReferenceError: myVariable is
                            not defined
```

To debug such errors, double-check variable names for typos and ensure that variables are declared and in the scope where they are accessed.

Type Errors

Type errors occur when an operation is performed on an inappropriate data type. This can include using methods or properties that do not exist for a particular type or attempting unsupported operations. Example:

```
const number = 42;
number.toUpperCase(); // TypeError: number.toUpperCase is not a
                                 function
```

Debugging Strategy: Review your code and ensure that you are using the appropriate methods and operations for the data types involved. Use `console.log` statements or a debugger to inspect the values and types of variables.

Logical Errors

Logical errors occur when the code does not produce the expected behavior or when there are flaws in the logical flow of your program. Example:

```
function calculateTotal(price, quantity) {
    return price + quantity; // Incorrect calculation
}
console.log(calculateTotal(10, 5)); // Output: 105
```

Debugging Strategy: Review your code's logic and verify your algorithms and formulas. Use `console.log` statements or a debugger to trace the values of variables and identify where the incorrect behavior occurs.

Logical errors cannot be identified by your Integrated Development Environment (IDE) or Appsmith's JavaScript editor, and can be the most difficult ones to debug. If you encounter unexpected behavior by your application and cannot figure out the reason, re-read the section "A Framework for Effective Bug Investigation" and employ the strategies described therein to dig out the root cause behind it.

Furthermore, JavaScript can be a tricky language to master if you have not programmed before. If you find yourself getting stuck with JavaScript while developing a complex Appsmith application, the authors recommend a book called *Eloquent JavaScript* by Marijin Haverbeke, available to read for free at `https://eloquentjavascript.net`. This book is intended for beginners to programming and JavaScript, and covers all the basic topics to help you understand the language and its syntax.

By understanding and recognizing these types of JavaScript errors, you can effectively debug your Appsmith applications. Strategies for debugging include reviewing code for syntax errors, carefully inspecting variable names and scopes, validating data types and operations, and using `console.log` statements or a debugger to track values and code flow. With these techniques, you'll be well equipped to identify and resolve JavaScript errors in your Appsmith applications.

Query Errors

While building Appsmith applications that interact with databases, you may encounter various types of SQL query errors. Understanding these errors and having effective debugging strategies will help you identify and resolve issues in your database queries. Let's explore some common SQL query errors you may encounter while building an Appsmith application.

Syntax Errors

Syntax errors occur when your SQL query violates the syntax rules of the database. These errors often result from missing or misplaced keywords, incorrect punctuation, or improper table or column references. Example:

```
SELECT *
FROM Users
WHERE name = John AND age > 30 -- Missing quotation marks
around "John"
```

To debug such errors, carefully review your SQL query and ensure proper syntax, including correct quoting, parentheses, and table/column names.

Incorrect Query Logic

Incorrect query logic refers to errors in the structure or logic of your SQL query that lead to unexpected or incorrect results. This can include incorrect join conditions, missing or incorrect WHERE clauses, or improper use of aggregate functions. Example:

```
SELECT COUNT(*)
FROM Orders
WHERE status = 'Pending' AND product_id = 123 -- Incorrect
filter condition
```

To debug such errors, review the logic of your SQL query, ensure the correct use of operators and conditions, and verify that the query matches your intended logic.

Mismatches between Query Parameters and Database Schemas

Mismatches between query parameters and database schemas occur when the parameters or variables used in your SQL query do not match the defined schema of the database table or column. This can lead to errors such as attempting to insert incompatible data types or referencing non-existent columns. Example:

```
INSERT INTO Customers (id, name, email)
VALUES (1, 'John Doe', 'john@example.com', '2021-01-01')
-- Excess value in the query
```

Debugging Strategy: Verify that the query parameters, variable values, and data types align with the database schema for the specific table or column being referenced.

Data Integrity Violations

Data integrity violations occur when your SQL query violates integrity constraints defined in the database schema, such as unique key constraints or referential integrity constraints. This can result in errors when inserting or updating data that conflicts with these constraints. Example:

```
INSERT INTO Employees (id, name, email)
VALUES (1, 'John Doe', 'john@example.com') -- Duplicate primary
key value
```

Debugging Strategy: Examine the integrity constraints defined in your database schema and ensure that your SQL queries adhere to these constraints.

There can be even more SQL-related errors that haven't been examined here. Fortunately, there are a lot of resources online where you can learn SQL and apply that knowledge to building your Appsmith applications. For beginners, the authors recommend SQL Bolt, available at `https://sqlbolt.com`, which contains a comprehensive set of interactive tutorials to help you master the language, completely free of charge.

By understanding these common SQL query errors, you can effectively debug and troubleshoot issues in your Appsmith applications. Strategies for debugging SQL query errors include carefully reviewing query syntax, validating query logic, ensuring parameter and variable alignment with database schemas, and verifying compliance with data integrity constraints.

Summary

In this chapter, we delved into the crucial topic of error handling and troubleshooting in Appsmith application development. We explored various aspects and techniques that empower developers to identify, diagnose, and resolve errors effectively. Let's recap the key takeaways from this chapter:

1. **Importance of Error Handling and Troubleshooting**: We emphasized the significance of error handling and troubleshooting in the development process. Understanding and resolving errors promptly ensures the stability and functionality of your Appsmith applications.

2. **Debugging Tools**: We discussed the essential tools for debugging, including the console object and the browser's debugger. These tools provide valuable insights into application behavior, variable values, code execution flow, and network interactions.

3. **Debugging Different Error Types**: We explored different error types, such as application errors, database errors, JavaScript errors, REST API errors, and SQL query errors. For each type, we provided insights into their causes, diagnostic approaches, and resolution strategies.

4. **Troubleshooting Best Practices**: We highlighted best practices for effective troubleshooting, such as following a systematic approach, maintaining logs and error tracking, and continuously learning and improving debugging skills.

By mastering the techniques and strategies discussed in this chapter, you are now well equipped to tackle errors and troubleshoot effectively in your Appsmith applications. Remember to reproduce issues, understand expected behavior, isolate problems, gather information, formulate hypotheses, and test and validate your solutions.

As you proceed with your application development journey, it is essential to maintain a proactive mindset in error handling. Embrace errors as opportunities for growth and learning. By continuously improving your debugging skills and staying up-to-date with best practices, you will become a more proficient Appsmith developer.

In the upcoming chapters, we will explore more advanced topics in Appsmith application development, empowering you to build powerful and robust low-code applications. Embrace the challenges that come with error handling and troubleshooting, as they will ultimately contribute to your growth as a developer. Happy debugging!

CHAPTER 8

Monitoring Appsmith

In the evolving landscape of low-code development platforms, Appsmith has distinguished itself as a formidable tool, offering unmatched flexibility and adaptability. Whether you're deploying a small application for internal use or rolling out a comprehensive suite for a large enterprise, the stability and performance of your Appsmith installation are paramount. This importance is accentuated when you opt for a self-hosted solution, placing the onus of upkeep and troubleshooting squarely on your shoulders.

Monitoring your Appsmith installation isn't just about ensuring everything is running smoothly; it's about being proactive, anticipating potential issues before they arise, and safeguarding the user experience. It's about maximizing uptime, maintaining optimal performance, and ensuring that you're always a step ahead of any challenges.

In this chapter, we'll dive deep into the nuances of monitoring a self-hosted Appsmith installation. From understanding the fundamental architecture to leveraging cutting-edge tools, we'll guide you through every step, ensuring that your monitoring approach is holistic, efficient, and effective. As you turn the pages, remember: a well-monitored application isn't just about troubleshooting; it's about delivering consistent value, achieving operational excellence, and building unwavering trust with your users.

© Rahul Sharma and Rajat Arora 2023
R. Sharma and R. Arora, *Low-Code Development with Appsmith*,
https://doi.org/10.1007/978-1-4842-9813-8_8

Monitoring Principles

At its core, monitoring is a proactive approach, a means to ensure the health, availability, and performance of your Appsmith installation. But before diving into the intricacies of monitoring Appsmith's architecture, it's crucial to understand the underlying principles of monitoring. These tenets lay the foundation for any robust monitoring strategy, ensuring you're not just collecting data, but gleaning actionable insights from it:

1. **Comprehensive Visibility:** The primary goal of monitoring is to obtain a clear and complete view of your system's state. This means observing not just the server's health but every component—from the frontend to databases and even third-party integrations. Comprehensive visibility ensures you catch anomalies at every layer, minimizing the risk of undetected issues.

2. **Proactivity over Reactivity:** Effective monitoring is about anticipating issues before they arise, not just reacting when they do. By setting up predictive alerts and understanding trends, you can address potential problems before they impact your users or escalate into bigger challenges.

3. **Baseline Establishment:** Before you can identify anomalies, you must understand what "normal" looks like for your system. By establishing a baseline—understanding average response times, CPU usage, memory consumption, etc.—you can easily spot deviations that might indicate problems.

4. **Granularity Matters:** While high-level metrics are essential for a general understanding, it's the granular, detailed data that often holds the key to diagnosing complex issues. Your monitoring tools and strategy should allow for both macro and micro views of your system.

5. **Adaptability:** Your Appsmith installation will evolve—new features, more users, changing workloads. Your monitoring strategy should be adaptable, capable of scaling, and flexible to adjust to these changes.

6. **Accessibility and Clarity:** Monitoring data is of little use if it's not easily accessible or understandable. Dashboards, visualizations, and clear metric representations are pivotal. Every stakeholder, from developers to system admins, should be able to glean insights without sifting through convoluted data.

7. **Automation:** In today's dynamic environments, manual monitoring is neither efficient nor effective. Leverage automation wherever possible, be it in data collection, anomaly detection, or even remedial actions.

8. **Regular Review:** Even with the most advanced tools, it's essential to periodically review your monitoring setup. This ensures that no new vulnerabilities have arisen and that your system is still aligned with the initial monitoring objectives.

9. **Continuous Learning:** Every alert, anomaly, or issue is an opportunity to learn. By analyzing these events, refining your alert thresholds, and understanding the root causes, you'll continually enhance your monitoring approach.

In essence, monitoring your self-hosted Appsmith installation isn't just about tools and metrics—it's about a mindset. By understanding and imbibing these principles, you set the stage for a resilient, efficient, and user-centric application environment. As we delve deeper into the subsequent sections, keep these tenets in mind to inform your strategies and decisions.

Overview of Appsmith Architecture

Appsmith, as you already know from reading the previous chapters, is an open-source, low-code software platform that empowers developers to build dashboards, forms, and various applications with speed and efficiency. Its architecture, though seemingly straightforward, is modular and scalable, ensuring adaptability for various use cases. For readers who've chosen to install Appsmith using its `docker-compose` file, this modular architecture is particularly evident.

Core Components

1. **Appsmith Server**: As the beating heart of your installation, the server manages the primary logic of Appsmith. It interacts with databases, processes API requests, and handles user authentication, among other tasks. Running within a Docker container, the server's performance and health are pivotal for the smooth functioning of your apps.

2.   **Front end**: This component drives the user interface
of Appsmith. Built primarily using React, it offers
a drag-and-drop interface where developers can
design and edit their applications. The front end
communicates directly with the server to fetch
or send data, ensuring real-time updates and
interactions.

3.   **MongoDB**: Appsmith uses MongoDB as its
primary database. This NoSQL database stores
application configurations, user data, and other vital
information. Ensuring its performance is crucial as
it directly impacts the responsiveness and efficiency
of the applications you've built.

4.   **Redis**: Used for caching and session management,
Redis improves performance by reducing the need
to repeatedly fetch data from the primary database.

5.   **NGINX**: Serving as a reverse proxy, NGINX ensures
seamless communication between the frontend
and the server, in addition to handling SSL
configurations and other network-related tasks.

Communication Flow

The synergy between these components is what makes Appsmith so
versatile. When a user interacts with an application (front end), a request is
sent to the Appsmith server, which might communicate with MongoDB or
make an external API call. Redis might step in if cached data can fulfill the
request. Finally, the response is routed back through NGINX to the user
interface, resulting in the desired action or update.

Following this interconnected dance of components, it's important to note that Appsmith simplifies the deployment process by encapsulating all these parts—NGINX, the Appsmith server, MongoDB, and Redis—into a single Docker container. This design choice is intended to streamline the installation and management processes, making it extremely convenient for end users to get an Appsmith instance up and running with minimal configuration and hassle.

However, this bundled approach presents a challenge when it comes to granular monitoring. Because all components are housed within a single container, you're essentially looking at a "black box," where it becomes difficult to separately monitor the health, performance, and logs of each individual component like MongoDB, Redis, or the Appsmith server itself. Instead, what you can generally monitor is the overall health and resource utilization of the Appsmith Docker container as a whole.

There's a silver lining to this challenge, though. Appsmith offers configuration options that allow you to specify external endpoints for MongoDB and Redis. When these external endpoints are provided, Appsmith will prioritize these connections over the internally housed copies of MongoDB and Redis. This means that instead of using the MongoDB and Redis instances that come bundled within the Docker container, the system will connect to the external databases that you specify.

This is a valuable feature for those who wish to monitor system components at a more granular level. By leveraging external instances of MongoDB and Redis, you have the freedom to monitor, manage, and scale these databases independently of the Appsmith container. This enables you to capture more detailed metrics, implement fine-grained security controls, and optimize resource utilization for these particular components.

Setting up Appsmith with externally sourced components is out of the scope of this book. However, you are free to peruse and implement the guide provided by Appsmith at `https://docs.appsmith.com/getting-started/setup/instance-configuration/custom-mongodb-redis`.

The Appsmith Monitoring Stack

Great, now that we've established the constraints and possibilities of monitoring within an Appsmith environment, let's dive into the tooling that will help us achieve our monitoring goals. We'll be utilizing three primary tools to monitor your Appsmith installation: cAdvisor, Prometheus, and Grafana. Each of these tools plays a unique role, and, when used in tandem, they provide a comprehensive monitoring solution.

cAdvisor (Container Advisor)

cAdvisor is an open-source tool that provides real-time monitoring and statistics for running Docker containers. Developed by Google, cAdvisor is designed to collect, process, and export information about running containers, providing details about resource usage and performance characteristics. With cAdvisor, you can quickly assess the CPU, memory, disk, and network statistics of your Appsmith container in real-time.

Prometheus

Prometheus is a powerful open-source monitoring and alerting toolkit originally built at SoundCloud. It features a multi-dimensional data model, a flexible query language, and integrates many aspects of systems and service monitoring. Its core component is a time-series database where it stores all the metrics data that gets scraped from the targets it monitors. Prometheus excels at reliability, allowing you to access data even during network outages and server crashes.

Grafana

Grafana is an open-source analytics and monitoring platform that integrates with a multitude of data sources, including Prometheus. It's known for its beautiful and informative dashboards where you can visualize complex queries and metrics. Grafana allows you to create, explore, and share dashboards with your team, fostering collaboration and facilitating quick decision making.

How They Work Together

1. **Data Collection**: cAdvisor will be our first line of defense, continuously monitoring the Appsmith Docker container and collecting real-time resource usage statistics.

2. **Data Storage**: Prometheus will be configured to scrape this real-time data from cAdvisor. It then stores this information in its time-series database, enabling historical analysis and alerting functionality.

3. **Data Storage**: Prometheus will be configured to scrape this real-time data from cAdvisor. It then stores this information in its time-series database, enabling historical analysis and alerting functionality.

By combining cAdvisor for immediate data collection, Prometheus for long-term storage and alerting, and Grafana for powerful visualizations, you can build a robust, comprehensive monitoring solution for your Appsmith installation. This trio of tools ensures that you not only understand what is happening in your system right now but also have the capability to analyze trends over time, which is invaluable for maintaining a healthy, efficient application environment.

Installing the Monitoring Stack

Great, let's move on to installation and configuration. One of the most convenient aspects of using Docker is the ability to manage multiple services using a single `docker-compose.yml` file. In this guide, we'll leverage this feature to install not just Appsmith but also cAdvisor, Prometheus, and Grafana for monitoring.

First, please stop the currently running Appsmith Docker container by running the following command in the directory where its `docker-compose.yml` file exists:

```
docker compose down
```

Once the containers have been stopped, you can modify your existing `docker-compose.yml` file to include the monitoring services. The following is the complete file that you should use:

```
services:
  appsmith:
    image: index.docker.io/appsmith/appsmith-ce
    container_name: appsmith
    ports:
      - 80:80
    volumes:
      - vl_appsmith:/appsmith-stacks
    networks:
      - nw_appsmith
    restart: unless-stopped
```

```
prometheus:
  image: prom/prometheus:latest
  container_name: prometheus
  ports:
  - 9090:9090
  command:
  - --config.file=/etc/prometheus/prometheus.yml
  volumes:
  - ./prometheus.yml:/etc/prometheus/prometheus.yml:ro
  networks:
  - nw_appsmith
  depends_on:
  - cadvisor
cadvisor:
  image: gcr.io/cadvisor/cadvisor:latest
  container_name: cadvisor
  ports:
  - 8080:8080
  volumes:
  - /:/rootfs:ro
  - /var/run:/var/run:rw
  - /sys:/sys:ro
  - /var/lib/docker/:/var/lib/docker:ro
  networks:
  - nw_appsmith
grafana:
  image: grafana/grafana-enterprise
  container_name: grafana
  restart: unless-stopped
  environment:
    - GF_INSTALL_PLUGINS=grafana-clock-panel
  ports:
```

```
    - 3000:3000
  volumes:
    - vl_grafana:/var/lib/grafana
  networks:
    - nw_appsmith
volumes:
  vl_grafana:
    external: true
  vl_appsmith:
    external: true
networks:
  nw_appsmith:
    external: true
```

Now, create another file called prometheus.yml and place it in the same directory as your docker-compose.yml. The prometheus.yml file will configure Prometheus to ingest data from Container Advisor every five seconds.

```
scrape_configs:
- job_name: cadvisor
  scrape_interval: 5s
  static_configs:
  - targets:
    - cadvisor:8080
```

Explanation of Major Parts of the Docker Compose File

The above docker-compose.yml deploys several components, with their respective configuration. Each of these components performs a specific function as outlined below:

- **Appsmith**: The appsmith service runs the main Appsmith application. It exposes it on port 80 and uses a named volume (vl_appsmith) for persistent storage.

- **Prometheus**: This service runs the Prometheus container, exposing it on port 9090. It uses a custom configuration file (`prometheus.yml`) that you'll place in the same directory as your `docker-compose.yml`.

- **cAdvisor**: This service is responsible for collecting container metrics. It exposes a web UI on port 8080 and collects metrics from various system locations, specified in the volumes.

- **Grafana**: The Grafana service runs the Grafana container, exposing it on port 3000. It uses a named volume (`vl_grafana`) for persistent storage.

- **Volumes and Networks**: The volumes and networks sections define the named volumes and networks that are used by the services. They're marked as external, which means they should already exist before running `docker-compose` up.

Why Use External Networks and Volumes?

External networks and volumes in Docker provide the following benefits:

1. **Isolation**: By defining an external network, you isolate your Appsmith and monitoring stack from other Docker networks. This ensures that your monitoring environment is secure and not influenced by other containers running on the same machine.

2. **Data Persistence**: Using external volumes ensures that data is persistent even if the containers are destroyed. This is particularly important for databases like Prometheus and Grafana, which need to maintain data across restarts for historical analysis.

3. **Resource Sharing**: External networks and volumes
   can be easily shared among multiple services or even
   different `docker-compose` setups, offering flexibility
   in multi-container or multi-service scenarios.

4. **DNS Resolution**: An additional advantage of using
   a user-defined network is that Docker provides
   automatic DNS resolution for container names. This
   is particularly useful in a microservices architecture
   like our Appsmith and monitoring stack, where
   services need to communicate with each other.

Before running your `docker-compose` command, you'll need to create
the specified external networks and volumes. If you don't do this, the
`docker compose up` command will throw an error, as it will not find the
declared external entities.

To create an external network named `nw_appsmith`, run the following
command:

```
docker network create nw_appsmith
```

To create external volumes named `vl_grafana` and `vl_appsmith`, use
the following commands:

```
docker volume create vl_grafana
docker volume create vl_appsmith
```

These commands will create a network and volumes that can be used
by the containers defined in your `docker-compose.yml` file.

Running Docker Compose

Once you've created the external network and volumes, you're ready to
bring your services up. Navigate to the directory containing your `docker-compose.yml` and run the following:

```
docker-compose up -d
```

235

This will pull the necessary Docker images and start the containers in detached mode, releasing the terminal after the operation.

You've now set up your Appsmith instance along with a powerful monitoring stack. In the next sections, we'll go into the configuration details for each service to ensure you're getting the most out of your monitoring setup.

Configuring Grafana

Container Advisor and Prometheus do not need extensive configuration. In fact, Container Advisor is practically plug-and-play. As soon as its container starts, it starts collecting data from all the running Docker containers in your system. Furthermore, the prometheus.yml file already instructs Prometheus to scrape data from Container Advisor. Now all that remains is to configure Grafana to show you some pretty graphs!

If everything is set up correctly, Grafana should be accessible to you at http://localhost:3000. For logging in the first time, you can input admin in both the username and password fields. (Be sure to change your password as soon as you log in).

Once logged in, the very first thing you will do is to create a data source.

Figure 8-1. *Adding your first data source in Grafana*

In the resulting screen, choose "Prometheus" from the Time Series Database section and configure its URL as http://prometheus:9090.[1] This is the only configuration you need to do. Scroll down and click on "Save and Test" to save the data source.

Now, to create a visualization, create your first dashboard from Grafana home screen (Figure 8-2).

Figure 8-2. *Creating a dashboard in Grafana*

Once you click on the tile, you will be presented with an empty dashboard. Click on "Create Visualization" to add your first panel to the dashboard. This will take you to a visualization configuration screen.

You can create a visualization by selecting a *metric*, filtering it for a particular *container*, and then adding a *range* operation over it. At the bottom of the empty panel, you will find options to configure all of these.

First of all, select a metric: container_cpu_system_seconds_total. In the Label Filters section, select Label = name and Value = appsmith. Then,

---

[1] Wondering about the weird URL? Well, due to all our containers present inside a user-defined Docker network, it provides automatic DNS resolution based on container names.

in the Operations section, select Range Functions ➤ Rate, and set the interval to be 1 minute (will be 1m in the dropdown). Finally, click on the "Run Queries" button to have the data plotted on the panel.

Depending on how long your Container Advisor and Prometheus containers have been running, you might only get a small number of data points as yet. However, this is a great start, and as you keep using your Appsmith installation, the metrics data will keep on accumulating and will give you insights on the health of your system (Figure 8-3).

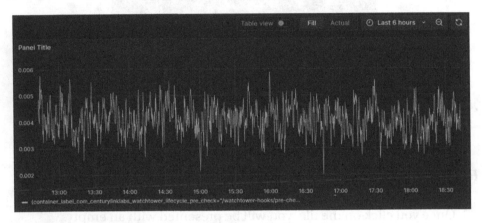

Figure 8-3.   *Your first Grafana visualization*

You can see a large number of available metrics in the Metrics dropdown. It includes metrics around CPU, memory, file system, and network traffic. All of this data has been collected by Container Advisor and persisted inside the Prometheus database. After saving this panel on your dashboard ("Save" button on the top-right corner), feel free to add more panels to it using different metrics as per your requirement.

Of course, this is not the only way to expose health metrics for your Appsmith container. If your organization uses container-based deployment methods, they likely already have a monitoring system in place. You can easily expose both container health metrics and container logs to systems like New Relic, Sumo Logic, Datadog, Splunk, etc. and use them to create health dashboards for Appsmith.

Working with Appsmith Cloud

When it comes to selecting software for their enterprise, it is crucial for organizations to comprehend the actual value that the software will bring to their business. It is not uncommon for companies to invest a significant amount of capital expenditure without adequately assessing the end objectives of the investment. This can result in costly buyer's remorse, negatively impacting strategic initiatives such as citizen development. With Software-as-a-Service (SaaS) platforms, organizations have the opportunity to validate the value-add of the software before committing to a purchase. These platforms offer a pay-as-you-go model that allows users to evaluate the benefits of the software empirically. While it is relatively easy to get started with SaaS platforms, it is important to note that there are challenges associated with operating in the cloud. Therefore, it is imperative to understand the requirements for working with Appsmith Cloud before diving in.

Appsmith Cloud

SaaS has become an essential aspect of the contemporary digital supply chain, and Appsmith is no exception. Appsmith offers its cloud services such that users can sign up, create applications, collaborate with others, and so forth. Appsmith Cloud is designed to cater to evaluators, experimenters, students, and the community, among others. The free version of Appsmith powers this cloud service, and users can expect the same set of features and functionality whether they opt for the SaaS or self-hosted deployment options. This presents an excellent opportunity to evaluate and validate the product and its integration with the enterprise application landscape. It is worth noting that the community version may lag behind the cloud release, meaning that a self-hosted instance may require features already present in the cloud version. This generally does not pose any significant issues, but users may need to make minor application modifications on the self-hosted instance.

Benefits

SaaS services have emerged as a game-changer in the world of enterprise solutions, offering unparalleled speed and agility without any significant lead time. Moreover, the citizen developer model reinforces the need for adaptable digital tools (LCDPs/NCDPs) for non-developers. These platforms must offer speed with a business's pace and evolving requirements. Thus, a SaaS offering for LCDPs looks like a good opportunity with a host of benefits that are worth noting.

One of the primary benefits of SaaS adoption is the reduced total cost of ownership. When evaluating a purchase decision, organizations typically compare the price of on-premises software with the recurring cost of an SaaS subscription. However, this comparison fails to capture the full spectrum of costs associated with on-premises solutions, such as support costs, additional hardware, personnel for maintenance and support, network monitoring, and management tools, among others. In contrast, many of these costs are included in the subscription cost of SaaS, leading to a lower total cost of ownership with reduced complexity and overhead.

Another noteworthy advantage of SaaS is the zero maintenance that it offers. On-premises software tends to age quickly, and getting the latest innovation often involves a time-intensive and costly upgrade process that may take at least a year. By contrast, SaaS users can always stay up-to-date with the latest version, with immediate access to new capabilities and features as soon as they become available. Being updated with the latest features ensures that your subscription actually appreciates over time, providing you with even more value.

Simply put, SaaS services offer many advantages that cannot be underestimated. Incorporating SaaS can significantly boost a company's ability to compete and adapt in a constantly evolving business landscape.

Challenges

When considering the adoption of Appsmith Cloud, it is vital to take into account potential risks that may arise. The cloud platform is used to develop applications based on user data that may only be accessible within your data center. As a result, Appsmith Cloud IP access may require inclusion in your database's allowlist. However, this may pose a challenge for highly regulated industries, such as banking and insurance, that prioritize data security and strive to minimize their security surface area. Additionally, adhering to data confidentiality constraints may limit access to sensitive data to the organization's private network, thus further complicating the process of granting Appsmith access.

Furthermore, it is crucial to note that if you choose to host your databases outside the U.S. regions, Appsmith Cloud may perform poorly. This is primarily because the data transfer would rely on the public network instead of a dedicated network. This makes it impossible to regulate the quality of service or equipment used. Additionally, transmitting unencrypted data over public networks can expose your data to various threats, such as data theft. While data encryption at the database level is feasible, this can pose its own problems and may require migration measures to ensure compatibility with existing business applications.

You must allow the IP addresses 18.223.74.85 and 3.131.104.27 before integrating your database in Appsmith Cloud.

You can also use API integration to work around the challenges faced with DB integration. You can load data using internal APIs, with authentication keys, invoked from the Appsmith domain. Another viable option is deploying a GraphQL engine, such as Hasura, to expose specific tables over APIs, with authentication. It is essential to note that these APIs are accessed via HTTPS, ensuring the secure transmission of data. Although data access may be slower than with DB integration, it presents an excellent opportunity for product evaluation. It is essential to carefully weigh the potential benefits and drawbacks before making the decision to adopt Appsmith Cloud.

Application access is another aspect that needs consideration while working in Appsmith Cloud. An Appsmith application can be classified as being either of two modes :

1. Private applications are restricted, with invite-only access to its users. All users must sign up on Appsmith Cloud and must be provided with an appropriate application role—viewer or developer

2. Private applications are restricted, with invite-only access to its users. All users must signup on to Appsmith Cloud and must be provided with an appropriate application role – viewer or developer

An application with private access would require the entire set of users to onboard Appsmith Cloud, which can significantly increase the subscription costs. However, public access applications pose a high risk as they can expose confidential business data online. Appsec teams must audit these public access applications before allowing production use.

After carefully considering the potential risks involved, it is recommended that an on-premises installation of the Appsmith community version is the best course of action. Moreover, if you are working with numerous teams, deploying the on-premises community version of the software is highly recommended for maximum security and peace of mind.

Summary

In this chapter, we embarked on a comprehensive journey to understand how to effectively monitor a self-hosted Appsmith installation. From getting an overview of Appsmith's architecture to diving into the principles of monitoring, we explored the various tools and techniques that can be deployed to keep tabs on your Appsmith instance's health and performance.

We specifically focused on the Docker-based installation of Appsmith and its unique challenges in monitoring due to its single-container deployment. A significant portion of this chapter was dedicated to understanding how to set up a monitoring stack using cAdvisor, Prometheus, and Grafana. We looked at how these tools complement each other and work in synergy to provide real-time and historical data, which can be visualized for better decision making.

We also touched upon the Appsmith Cloud, discussing its benefits and challenges. While cloud offerings usually come with built-in monitoring solutions and easy-to-use interfaces, they often may not meet specific requirements, especially when it comes to handling sensitive or confidential data. The flexibility and control offered by a self-hosted instance are unparalleled in this respect.

In the end, monitoring is not just about collecting data; it's about making that data actionable. The insights gathered can help you not only react to issues quickly but also proactively manage your Appsmith instance, ensuring it is secure, resilient, and optimized for performance. Armed with the knowledge from this chapter, you are now better prepared to take your Appsmith deployment to the next level of operational excellence.

CHAPTER 9

Implementation Patterns with Appsmith

Appsmith is a versatile platform that allows developers to create applications with speed and adaptability. It provides the ability to integrate multiple databases and orchestrate external APIs for various workflows. Additionally, Appsmith supports the creation of multiple application pages and the execution of parallel transformations—with fallbacks for business resilience. However, to get the most out of Appsmith, it is vital to follow specific best practices. Adhering to these principles is critical for avoiding common pitfalls that can arise when working with the platform. They also help to reduce the likelihood of runtime issues and maintainability problems. By sticking to these guidelines, developers can implement proven methods for solving common issues efficiently and effectively.

Implementing best practices is also vital in improving application performance and speeding up development time. By following these guidelines, developers can prevent common coding errors and boost their application's performance. The low-code patterns discussed in this chapter are aimed to support fast, scalable, and reliable methods for reading and processing data. By leveraging these patterns, developers can create high-quality applications that meet their users' needs.

UI Patterns

An application's user experience (UX) is vital in determining its success. It is impacted by various factors, such as functionality, usability, and engagement. One of the most effective ways to create a great UX is by incorporating user interface (UI) patterns that prioritize a content-first approach. This involves placing the application's content at the forefront of the design and building the UI around it. By doing so, you can create a seamless and enjoyable experience for users that is both intuitive and engaging. This approach ensures that users can easily access the information they need without getting bogged down by unnecessary clutter or distractions. Ultimately, this will lead to higher engagement rates and increased user satisfaction, which are crucial for the long-term success of any application.

Multi-page Application

Web application performance is often measured by the page load time. The faster an application loads, the more engagement it has from the user. However, slow-loading applications provide a poor user experience and struggle in gaining user adoption. Thus, you must understand issues affecting the application page load time so that accurate optimization and fixes can be developed.

In Appsmith, a single-page application can exhibit slow performance. Your dashboard application might have tables, charts, metrics, and scripts that are fetching data from various sources. The data shown on the page is often fetched at page load, and multiple query executions can adversely affect the page load. You can improve application load time by breaking these flows across several pages. The application's default page will execute fewer queries, loading only limited data and loading faster. Moreover, the application navigation menu will execute queries corresponding to individual pages. Creating a multi-page app can also result in reduced maintenance effort as each page can have the corresponding application logic rather than having all on one single page.

Creating multiple pages is one of many ways of improving performance. Your goal is to reduce the number of queries on page load. You can achieve this by using several other components, like dropdowns, tabs, modals, etc. Queries can be executed on several event handlers like OnClick to load the required data. If there are several interdependent queries, they can be executed in a chain according to user input.

A multi-page application can yield performance benefits, but breaking data across several pages must be thought through. It is not a panacea for all data-loading issues, as keeping certain things on the same page can have advantages. All data relating to the most important features of the page must be fetched on the same page rather than loading the same data twice across pages.

Load data on demand. Fetch only the minimum data you need for the essential features of the page. Delegate non-related features to other pages.

Information Passing

Multi-page applications need to display the same information across several pages. Thus, you must plan to share the required data appropriately instead of fetching it again. Appsmith provides the following ways of sharing data across pages:

- URL query parameters

- Local storage

Let's run through how and when to use each and how to use these tools effectively.

Data can be passed as part of the URL using query parameters, which are a set of arguments and values appended to provide additional information to a given URL. These parameters can be consumed within the page using the Appsmith JS object `appsmith.URL.queryParams.argName`. The `navigateTo` method provides support (Figure 9-1) for passing these arguments to the respective page URL.

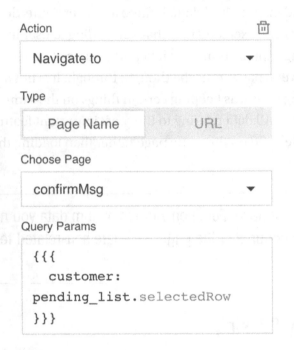

Figure 9-1. navigateTo method query args

It is crucial to understand that URLs and query parameters are not secure measures to share sensitive or critical information. The inclusion of confidential data like user identifiers, passwords, static shared secrets, or private data in such contexts is highly risky. This can lead to issues as users might share the page URL without realizing the confidential data it contains.

Applications can also use local storage to share information between pages. Local storage provides browser-based persistence that can be used to store key–value pairs without any expiration date. Appsmith provides the storeValue API (Figure 9-2) to accomplish this. A stored key can then be retrieved by using the appsmith.store.key property. Since this is persistent storage, the data remains intact and accessible across multiple reads without the need to refresh/rewrite it.

Figure 9-2. storeValue API for localstorage

Dynamic Rendering

Conditions provide the foundation for developing application workflows. Conditional rendering is an essential feature that enables the creation of UI components based on business logic, rendering only the necessary details. This capability empowers developers to build dynamic user interfaces that can adapt and respond to changes in data and user interactions. By strategically showing or hiding content based on user actions or the application state, developers can create more intuitive and engaging user experiences. The following are a few examples of this:

- Display different messages to the user based on the user's login status. This message is evaluated based on the `isLoggedIn` status for the user.

- Change the available actions based on the selected employee record (Active / Closed).

- Strikeout or highlight items in the ToDo list based on its completion.

Implementing conditional statements can significantly improve the effectiveness of the code and promote the development of modular components. This is accomplished by allowing the display of certain content while avoiding the repetition of code, which can lead to errors and decreased efficiency. By utilizing conditional statements, programmers can create more streamlined and organized code that is easier to maintain and update in the future.

Conditional rendering is often accomplished using ternaries. They work like `if/else` statements: these ternaries check if the first statement is true (the selected row = 'offline') and perform the action after the question mark (changing the text or color). If the statement is false (i.e., the selected row = 'online'), it performs the action after the colon. They can be used for almost everything, rending UI labels, controlling component styles (Figure 9-3), disabling fields, adding query arguments, and more.

CONTENT   STYLE

General

Button Variant `JS`

```
{{ appsmith.store?.jwt ? "PRIMARY" :"SECONDARY" }
```

Icon

Color

Button Color `JS` ●

```
{{ appsmith.store?.jwt ? "#818cf8" :"#553DE9" }}
```

Border and Shadow

Border Radius `JS` ●

```
{{ appsmith.store?.jwt ? "0px" : "1.5rem" }}
```

Figure 9-3. *Using ternary operator*

Dynamic Forms

Building forms involves a lot of copy and pasting of code. You need to add similar elements (maybe validations as well) and then rename them individually. It would be nice to automate some of the form creation process. The JSON form component covered in Chapter 3 provides several advantages. One advantage is that the code of the form is less verbose. You do not have to define multiple inputs in a single form. Another advantage is that controls can be generated dynamically. This is quite useful in master dataset use cases responsible for maintaining data. You can either use a static configuration containing (Figure 9-4) the uber list of fields or generate it dynamically based on the selected records.

Source Data

```
{
  "name": "John",
  "date_of_birth": "20/02/1990",
  "contact" : {
    "Phone": 999999999,
    "Email" : "user1@example.com"
  },
  "education" : {
    "institute" : "School Name",
    "level" : "PostGraduate"
  }
}
```

Figure 9-4. *Nested JSON form*

There are also some drawbacks, though. It takes more work to apply styles to the layout of your form. You may not be able to freely arrange the controls in the way you want. Using complex validations for each rule may also take a lot of work to implement.

Query Patterns

In today's digital age, data plays a crucial role in the success of any application. It is imperative that data is accessed quickly and securely to ensure the best possible user experience. However, poorly developed queries can have a detrimental impact on data processing. They can cause slow execution, resulting in inconsistent data, and may even lead to the loss of confidential information. Therefore, it is essential to follow best practices when it comes to data processing to ensure the highest level of security and efficiency.

Use Prepared Statements

Queries are executed to add, update, or read data from the database. Moreover, each query must conform to the syntax the corresponding database supports. Relational databases like MySQL PostgreSQL require queries in SQL format. These can be formed dynamically, constructed using string concatenation, or in prepared statement format, a template query with value parameters. Prepared statements are recommended while processing data provided by the application user either as direct input fields or derived fields from selected records. Prepared statements offer the following benefits:

Security

Proper data validation is essential to prevent SQL injection. Malicious attackers may attempt to insert valid SQL statements as user data inputs. These non-sanitized inputs can alter the query logic and result in unauthorized access to sensitive and confidential data. Therefore, it is essential to implement appropriate data validation and sanitization measures to safeguard against such attacks.

PreparedStatement provides numerous methods to pass parameters rather than concatenating the values to a query string. It allows your code to automatically escape special characters, such as quotations within the passed-in SQL statement. Thus, any attempts of encoding hacks or SQL hacks will not affect the structure of a query. This means that the query's logic remains uncompromised whether or not it produces a result set.

Efficiency

Another benefit of a prepared statement is that the SQL itself is pre-compiled a single time and then retained in the cache. Dynamic queries are compiled every time the statement is called. The database also caches the query plan for a prepared statement. It enables the Database to execute parameterized prepared statements queries much faster than dynamic queries. Thus, prepared statements provide performance benefits by offloading repetitive processing, mainly when performed several times.

Prefer prepared statements over dynamic SQL and disabled it only when necessary.

Batch Inserts

Some applications like admin panels may need to insert large sets of data, e.g., onboarding a new tenant or a product catalog. In such scenarios, creating records one at a time can be inefficient. RDBMS like MySQL and PostgreSQL provides a batch insert feature for such needs. Batch insert allows submitting multiple inserts to a single table, once to the database as a single `insert` statement instead of individual statements. This method improves latency and data insert times.

Appsmith's query interface does not support batch inserts out-of-the-box. But you achieve the same by executing a small JS function to create a batch insert query. The approach of batch insert consists of the following steps:

- Buffer the batch records, consisting of all required data values, in a JS array object.

- Pass the JS array object to the query execution. This can be done by either a query parameters or by using local storage.

- Iterate over the array and concatenate the values to generate a dynamic SQL.

```
Insert into users ('name', 'gender', 'age')
values
{{
appsmith.store.users.map((user) => { return "('" +
user.name + "'," + "'" + user.gender + "'," + "'"
+ user.age + "')" })
    .join(",")
}}
```

You should enable JDBC batching for write-most applications, as the performance benefits might be staggering.

Transactions

One distinguished feature of RDBMS systems is the ability for applications to update multiple items simultaneously through the use of transactions. Transactions allow a series of operations to be executed as a single unit of work. This ensures that either all operations are completed successfully or none are applied to the database. By doing so, transactions guarantee the consistency and integrity of data even in case of system failures. Overall, Transactions offer an essential tool for maintaining high levels of data reliability.

Appsmith does not support transactions out of the box. However, a few workarounds can be used to maintain data integrity. You can set up a chain of multiple queries to run "On Success" of one another so that if one fails, the remainder of the chain will not be run. Unfortunately, this does not undo the previous queries like rolling back a transaction does. You can also use On Failure hooks to execute rollback queries. But the approach can lead to a fragile and difficult-to-maintain system.

Databases also provide the concept of stored procedures. A stored procedure is a compiled program that can execute SQL statements and is stored in the database. The stored procedure accepts input and output parameters, executes the SQL statements, and returns a result set, if any. A procedure issues a `BEGIN`, `COMMIT`, or `ROLLBACK` statement within the procedure body; all changes made before the transaction statement are committed or rolled back, and the system implicitly starts a new transaction. All statements after the transaction command continue running as a single multi-statement command, not as individual commands inside a transaction block. Any uncommitted changes are committed or rolled back when the stored procedure exists. Stored procedures are invoked using the `CALL` statement:

```
CALL insert_movie_data("Comedy","Catch-22", 1.5);
SELECT 1 from DUAL;
```

Additionally, Appsmith requires a dummy `select` statement after the stored procedure invocation. The dummy statement ensures that any values returned by the stored procedure are captured by Appsmith and forwarded to the application.

JS Patterns

JavaScript patterns are a highly useful set of abstract concepts, viewpoints, and ideas that can be applied to a wide range of programming situations. Rather than offering specific approaches or methodologies, these patterns are designed to provide programmers with a streamlined approach to optimizing and maintaining their code.

Over the years, JavaScript has evolved significantly as a programming language, incorporating a variety of new ES specifications. This has created new opportunities for programmers to tackle problems in unique and inventive ways using the latest tools and techniques. By mastering the principles, programmers can take full advantage of these new capabilities and deliver high-quality code that meets the business needs.

Update Value of Input Fields

Input fields play a crucial role in user interface design as they provide a means of capturing user responses. These fields have multiple functions, such as displaying existing data, recording user inputs, validating application-derived data, and more. Typically, changes to the input data are captured using a callback handler, which is then used to perform business logic based on the updated information. Additionally, computed values can be displayed in other input fields to allow users to validate the processed data. For example, entering a zip code can automatically display the corresponding city name in the address details.

However, it's important to note that the current version of Appsmith does not support the update value feature. This feature may be available in future versions. The following workaround can be employed in the meantime to achieve the desired result:

- Assign a default value to the Input field using a local storage key. `{{ appsmith.store?.cityname }}`

- Capture the value of the preceding key by using StoreKey API as part of a separate JS function.

- Reset the required Input field using `resetWidget`, after successfully saving the key.

```
setCity (zipCode) {
  return zipcode_api.run({"zip": zipCode})
      .then(cityname => storeValue("city",
      cityname, false))
      .then(resetWidget('AddressCityInput'));
}
```

> The preceding method can be used to set values for several components, like button names, text labels, date fields, rating values, etc.

Asynchronous Callback Chains

In JavaScript, asynchronous code handling was achieved using a callback function. The purpose of this function was to execute after an asynchronous operation was completed. While this method worked as intended, it had its shortcomings. Coding with numerous callback functions could be challenging to read and maintain. Heavily nested callbacks were referred to as "callback hell." The term refers to areas within a codebase that may contain hidden and unexpected bugs, making it challenging to ensure the quality and stability of the product.

Promise

The introduction of promises addressed the callback hell problem. In JavaScript, a promise is an object that holds the future value of an asynchronous operation. It enables you to attach handlers to the eventual success value or failure reason of an asynchronous action (using the then method). The promise API lets you return another promise at the eventual completion. Thus, there is the concept of promise chains, where multiple promises can be executed one after another.

```
function onboardNewCustomer()
{
 return getCustomerDetails()
 .then(customer => { return getPaymentDetails(customer); })
 .then(pymtDetails => { return findNearbyStores(customer); })
 .then(store => { return generateWelcomeKit(customer,
 pymtDetails, store); })
```

```
.then(greetMsgDetails => { return sendComms(greetMsgDetails,
customer); })
}
```

This promise chaining is an improvement over callback hells. However, it does not entirely address the issue of code maintenance. Long promise chains can be challenging to understand and maintain.

Async and Await

Async and await is a new syntax that supports asynchronous invocations. The syntax provides a new, friendlier way of defining asynchronous callbacks, making them easier to understand and maintain. Instead of chaining promises together, Async and Await allows developers to write code that looks like synchronous code. Async and await implicitly use promises and make working easier.

```
function onboardNewCustomer()
{
  let customer = await getCustomerDetails ();
  let pymtDetails = await getPaymentDetails (customer);
  let stores = await findNearbyStores (customer);
  let food = await generateWelcomeKit (customer, pymtDetails,
  stores);
  return await sendComms (greetMsgDetails, customer);
}
```

Promises are a great way of writing concise code and handling ad hoc asynchronous operations. However, Async Await can be preferred for complex asynchronous operations.

Summary

In this chapter, a comprehensive discussion was held on the best practices to be followed while developing applications with Appsmith. These guidelines are primarily focused on building efficient, maintainable, and secure applications. The chapter covered a range of guidelines, each specific to Appsmith widgets, queries, and JavaScript executions. Each of these practices revolves around a particular component or feature covered in detail in the previous chapters:

- The UI practices discussed in the chapter aimed to solve the UX issues and render the UI quickly and effectively. These guidelines ensure that the application's user interface is responsive and easy to use, enhancing the user experience.

- The query patterns described in the chapter outlined ways to avoid inconsistent data, which is a critical aspect of application development. By following these guidelines, developers can ensure that the data critical to the application is accurate and consistent.

- The JS patterns discussed in the chapter aimed to improve the code's quality and maintainability. By following these guidelines, developers can enhance the overall quality of the codebase while making it more manageable.

The chapter presents ways of solving the most common issues while working with the different components, helping developers to avoid common pitfalls and improve application stability and performance.

Index

A

© Rahul Sharma and Rajat Arora 2023
R. Sharma and R. Arora, *Low-Code Development with Appsmith*,
https://doi.org/10.1007/978-1-4842-9813-8

Printed in the United States
by Baker & Taylor Publisher Services